Rory's GLORY

Design and layout: Alex Young

Publishers: Edward Adams and Jules Gammond for G2 Rights Ltd

First published in the UK in 2014 by G2 Rights Ltd,
Unit 7, Whiffens Farm, Clement Street, Hextable, Kent, BR8 7PQ

The right of Justin Doyle to be identified as the author of this book has been
asserted by them in accordance with the Copyright, Designs and Patents Act 1988.

Printed and bound in Europe

ISBN: 978-1-782811-30-5

The views in this book are those of the author but they are general views only and
readers are urged to consult the relevant and qualified specialists for individual advice in
particular situations.

G2 Entertainment hereby exclude all liability to the extent permitted by law of any
errors or omissions in this book and for any loss, damage or expense (Whether direct or
indirect) suffered by a third party relying on any information contained in this book.

Rory's GLORY

Written by
Justin Doyle

Foreword by
Tony Jacklin

G2 entertainment

CONTENTS

RORY'S DRIVER!

Belgium, March 2012

Dear Mr. Doyle,

I have read your book 'Rory, His Story So Far' with great interest and pleasure.

To be honest, before September last year I did notice Rory arriving on the golf scene but when watching golf on TV, I took more interest in Tiger Woods and at a later stage Lee Westwood. But even of those players I have never read any book or followed them via Facebook or Twitter.

Since September I am following 'Rors' in almost every manner. Why? During the KLM Open of 2011 I had the honour of being his dedicated chauffeur from Wednesday to Sunday. Although the playing schedule was terribly affected by the bad weather (rain and later thunderstorms), the organization did very well to manage the tournament over four days. This affected Rory's plans to have dinner and a visit to Amsterdam for which he asked me for some advice I even checked restaurants.

What amazed me was how mature he was for 22 years of age and how down to earth he was in all ways. In fact with his cap on, he almost looked shy. I was impressed from day one and when reading your book everything was confirming my impression of Rory McIlroy. Obviously during our 15 minute drive to and from the hotel we did not have lengthy discussions! But only some exchange of remarks; as a driver you are expected not to interfere or 'only talk when being talked to'. But the few remarks were pleasant and more than enough to have some impression.

I think ISM did a great job guiding and protecting Rory in a way that allowed him to grow up as a person he is now. Keeping him away from the media in his younger years was an appropriate thing to do. When you are at the age of Lee Westwood or Luke Donald then you can leave them to handle the media, not when you are in your early twenties.

Chapter 10 was well written: Controversies. Everybody is allowed to have his opinion and sometimes it is better to count to 10 before speaking out. I think Rory is still learning but instead of reacting in the media, more and more he lets his game of golf speak! I am looking forward to his encounters with Tiger and their meeting gave me great pleasure: their smiles on their face enjoying the game and having respect for each other.

Last but not least, I do not know whether you keep contact with Rory or his parents but whenever I see him on television, my family and me are proud to have met him.

Thank you very much for the creation of this book, hope there are many more to follow.

Kind regards,

Henri Vermeesch

FOREWORD

by Tony Jacklin CBE

Simply put, I see Rory McIlroy as a prince of a young man. He is intelligent; he seems to have a wonderful strength of mind and a clear sense of purpose. He always has time for people and, in terms of golfing ability, Rory has everything.

He is a tremendous tee-to-green player and is one of the best drivers of the ball I have seen – and believe me, I have seen a few. That combination of long and straight makes the game a lot easier for him and I see no reason why he cannot reach double figures in his quest for Major glory. Equally, if he looks after himself, I can see him completing the Grand Slam with a win at Augusta in the not too distant future.

People have, on occasion, made comparisons between Rory and myself. We both hail from the British Isles and left these shores to test ourselves in the States at an early age. We were both eager to learn at that stage and success visited us both pretty quickly. However, Rory inhabits a very different golfing environment to the one I found myself in back in the 1960s.

I was one of a small number of foreign players in the US and the Americans resented our presence and made life as difficult as they could for us. Of course, the likes of Jack Nicklaus and Arnold Palmer were different and ready to take us on in a sporting fashion but Rory faced different challenges when he first went over the pond.

The US Tour is much more welcoming nowadays, with a third of its players coming from overseas, but the attention from the media and the pressure that brings with it are intense. As a talented lad, things were expected of Rory from the outset but he committed fully and chose to make his move to America permanent. That is something I should have done all those years ago so it is good to see him learning from the experiences of others.

Rory has achieved great things already and clearly has time on his side. I doubt very much, however, that he will be thinking that way. I can see he wants to get stuck in and take things as far as he can. He knows the ball is in his court, so to speak, and that he must stay hungry.

From what I hear, he seems to be surrounding himself with the right kind of people, the ones with his best interests at heart, and his father is rightly at the centre of that.

He has also learnt at a young age that he does not have to play every single week and seems to appreciate the need for balance in his life. He reminds me of Nicklaus in that way. Jack never risked burn-out because he took breaks from playing to raise his family and design a course or two.

By maintaining a similar balance Rory can hold on to his hunger, specifically target the Majors and hopefully cement his name in golf history.

As humans we are all vulnerable and mistakes or misjudgments can be made but, if Rory can stay free from injury and keep the fire in his belly, he has the world at his feet.

He has come along at the right time and, although you should never write off Tiger, Rory is more than capable of taking on his mantle and establishing a lasting dominance in this game we all love.

I wish this young and highly talented Northern Irishman every bit of luck in fulfilling his extraordinary potential.

INTRODUCTION

Before I began putting pen to paper on my first biography of Rory McIlroy, entitled 'Rory – His Story So Far', I ventured up to his home town of Holywood, just outside Belfast in Northern Ireland.

I wanted to get a feel for everything Rory. What he saw when he grew up in the area, what sort of golf course he trawled with his father as a boy, the local shops (and even the bars!) he would have frequented, and I also took in the local school he attended.

In actual fact, Sullivan Upper High School was one of my first ports of call, and on the day I travelled there I just missed meeting Rory himself! When I went into the school's main hall it was still stuffy and very warm from a big welcome home party for him.

The school's most famous and favourite son had just won his first major – the US Open. High above the rows and rows of (by now empty) seats were banners reading 'Congratulations Rory', and I cursed my luck that I had missed an opportunity to say hello.

A few days later, I began work on what eventually turned out to be a very proud assignment. In managing to get the legendary Gary Player to write the foreword, the icing topped the cake.

The book began with my referring to the abundance of holly trees which grow in a wooded area at Glenlyon, which is just 500 metres walk uphill off the town's main street and so, rather appropriately, the name 'Holywood' was formed.

The picturesque golf course, which overlooks Belfast Harbour and its towering Harland & Wolffe cranes, is actually very tough looking and (for want of better words to describe 'hilly') very undulating.

H&W also served to remind us that this company gave much needed employment to many Northern Ireland families down through the decades. Rory's grandfather even worked those famous Belfast docks which would later launch the ill-fated Titanic.

Rory's family were directly affected by 'The Troubles'. An uncle of his was murdered, and that turbulent time is probably an underlying reason why he has clearly distanced himself from England and Ireland – he is staunchly Northern Ireland.

This in mind, it was then time to concentrate on the all-important business of golf and Rory's early days. His glittering early career was delved into, his time as an amateur at boys and youth level culminating in him becoming world champion at the Doral under-12s tournament in Florida.

His first European win as a pro in Dubai is remembered and proudly framed upstairs in the Holywood clubhouse. A memento of his first trip to the US Masters is also present on the wall with a famous yellow flag from a hole at Augusta that he eagled!

All the glorious details of his US Open win (as well as the trauma of his Masters meltdown) were covered and a book about anyone's life would not be a complete, or a fair assessment, if controversies were not dealt with – and they were.

So akin to a doctor getting a sense of his patient's wellbeing by observation, the trip north, as well as all the subsequent research, proved very worthwhile. Many pinpoint and accurate readings and predictions emanated from the start to the finish of that book.

Gary Player's opening foreword was a case in point. When I was a kid, I worshipped this golfer simply because my father so admired him. Player was small and slim in stature and I loved his immaculate jet-black polo neck and slacks and his lighter coloured caps.

To have him write the foreword was a fantastic honour but what he said in his piece was even more apt and pertinent. He talked about the differences between golf in his time and now.

He talked about how golf, back then, was a means to earning a living for him and his family, in contrast to the modern age where there is so much money about; how the media were a big part of the close-knit golfing tour party, which is not the case today.

Today's media, he said, are in search of salacious stories, and Rory would become all too aware of that. He would have to deal with all of this and a lot more pressure while still being expected to win majors consistently and become one of the best players in the game.

His final words were the most telling:

Rory, YOU have the game, now go out and show the world that you have the desire. Remember, 'the harder you practise the luckier you get'.

I will refer back to those final words of Gary's in a few moments but there were some sentiments of my own from the first book which were to prove correct – and others that were just a little off the mark!

The book went to press in November 2011 with the publishers receiving my completed manuscript by 1 October. On page 113, in the opening line of chapter nine 'Root of the Problem', I wrote:

If there is one major besides the US Open that Rory McIlroy seems destined to win, it is the USPGA.

Ten months later, and after playing in three preceding majors without any success, Rory did indeed win that USPGA. In fact, he won his second major with ease and by the exact same winning margin as his first major US Open triumph – eight shots.

Other notable things were talked about and came to pass. There was the question of his 'patriotic allegiances' towards either Team GB or Ireland which, just a few months into 2102, really took off in a huge way with the worldwide media.

The pressure Rory endured during that entire episode, until he finally made a decision in the summer of 2014, was immense. In fact it was so tough that Graeme McDowell pleaded with authorities to make the decision for Rory, citing the huge strain and effect.

In this book his wins, as well as the highs and lows of 2012 and 2014, will be dealt with. But sandwiched in between both of those seasons was a 2013 bereft of big successes and replaced by a total loss of top form.

So much so that Rory, for all his genius and God-given golf talents, had serious doubts whether he would ever reach the heady heights of major glory again. Be under no other illusions – 2013 was a very worrying time.

This period, which I cover in this book under the chapter entitled 'The Doldrums', left the sporting public with grave doubts about McIlroy's merits as a future superstar of world golf.

There was no way he could emulate or eclipse the great Tiger Woods with his sudden downturn in top form. Suddenly, from the best from of his life to the worst, a wave of pessimism pervaded concerning Rory.

Accompanying that pessimism was a large scale feeling that he was now just a 'good time Charlie' enjoying and revelling in his romance with Caroline Wozniacki. Rory was making all the headlines off the course with very little to be said about him on it.

If it was not photographs or headlines of Rory in happy times at parties or away on holiday breaks with his beloved, then it was more worrying headlines of impending doom which made the news.

Missing cuts did not help his new multi million-dollar Nike contract and his switchover to using their clubs. As if the pressure of that was not bad enough, well known golfers were coming out in the media stating Rory had erred and could not get used to new clubs.

After leaving Chubby Chandler to join Horizon Sports Management (with whom he hit the ground running) and everything seeming so rosy in the garden, he then left them amid a legal dispute which looked likely to be settled in the highest courts in the land.

Everything golf related seemed to be crumbling and collapsing around him. His 'blitzkrieg' form that won him two majors by eight shots was nowhere to be seen; he was missing cuts, he was missing months – but worse, he was fun-loving away on holidays!

All of these were precise echoes of what Gary Player had talked of in his foreword - public and media scrutiny, intrusion, constant pressure and the need to practise hard and make huge sacrifices.

Just when it seemed as if he would be an 'also-ran', content, as Player said in his piece, 'to settle for winning every once in a while', he answered what Gary (and Jack Nicklaus and the golfing Gods) had been seeking from Rory.

Off the golf course, and totally out of the blue, the need for ultimate sacrifice and hard practise was delivered by him in a most shocking and emphatic way to a worldwide audience.

It was THE building block he needed to single-handedly put in place a new construction of Rory Phase Two – and put it in place he did. Enjoy reading the story and reconstruction of an all new tower of strength.

Chapter 1

SPLITTING FROM WESTY & CHUBBS

After the highs and lows of 2011 – the US Open win which followed his US Masters meltdown – another whirlwind of a rollercoaster ride befell Rory at the end of that season and into 2012.

On the face of it, statistics may point to Rory McIlroy having a fantastic end to 2011. However, behind the facts of his unbelievably brilliant purple patch, lies a story of what might have been amid all the frustrating near misses.

Add to that the hectic end-of-season schedule of golf tournaments all over the world – the constant travelling, catching up on much needed sleep in jets and hotels, eating and drinking on the move – and a big crash of some sort was awaiting Rory around the bend.

Let us not forget Rory was also a young adult dating tennis player Caroline Wozniacki. There were a lot of tournaments where Rory literally dashed from the clubhouse to catch a flight to rendezvous with her.

His destination was either to a tennis event she was playing in, to her home in Monaco or to some romantic holiday destination. It seemed on the outside as if Rory was enjoying sheer bliss. But there was one big question: was his golf suffering as a result of all this?

Perhaps not towards the end of that season, but before that, and after, many big names in the world of golf were criticising him heavily for it. It was just the start of a period of upheaval, uncertainty and great changes going on in his life – on and off the golf course.

Ultimately McIlroy is programmed very well. He knows what he wants and will do anything required to achieve his goals. Even if it means making huge changes in his personal and personnel life – and cutting long lasting ties – he won't shy away.

Nor will he dwell on the matter for any lengthy period. When he makes up his mind his actions are swift and instantaneous. Upsets in his life, which sometimes may cause him to lose form, do not last very long.

Rory seems to sense when he goes too far and overdoes things. Unlike someone who has had too much to drink and then spoils things for himself and others, he has this inbuilt mechanism which knows how to pull back from the brink of disaster and fix the problem.

In that respect he has consistently shown two main ways where he puts things right:

(i) He desists from being in the company of an individual or individuals, meaning a split
(ii) He employs/enlists an individual or individuals to help him in an area of concern

He first illustrated this in mid-October 2011 when leaving his management company International Sports Management (ISM), run by Andrew 'Chubby' Chandler. It was a massive shock and it took the golfing world completely by surprise.

Behind the 'thanks for all the help' and 'I wish him all the best for the future' compliments and niceties which are almost always dished out when vacating a top position, nobody ever really knows the real reasons why sports stars (or others) leave a team.

The media will always surmise that it is mostly to do with money, contracts and working conditions. Sometimes though, it may go deeper and bears no relation to material things. Furthermore, Chubby Chandler and Rory McIlroy were a successful and winning team.

Who knows, but sometimes a golf genius like Rory, who is blessed with a great brain and vision, may see dangers down the line that he wants to steer clear of. It could have been that remaining in a stable with Westwood and Schwartzel was just not for him.

South African Charl Schwartzel was the player who stole Rory's thunder at the Masters, his outrageous chips and putts winning him the Green Jacket. Could Rory remain in ISM with Schwartzel's star rising? That is not to mention the Westwood factor.

Lee Westwood and Chubby are great buddies and their professional and personal relationship stretches back decades. A bit like the headmaster and his classroom pet, Westy was always top dog in the stable until Rory became the huge rising star.

In the weeks before the sensational split, Westwood and McIlroy engaged in a bit of friendly banter on twitter. At least, that is the way it seemed, until Westwood started that typical British trait of mickey-taking, and perhaps some of it irked Rory.

When Westy also brought up Chubby's name, perhaps Rory sensed that he would never really get the respect and recognition that he fully deserved as a major winner – something Lee Westwood has yet to achieve. One quip from Westwood read: 'You hear that, Chubbs – he's even beginning to talk like Wozniacki now'" (referring to the fact that Rory showed the world the bond developing between him and tennis girlfriend Caroline Wozniacki by having 'Wozzilroy' engraved on his clubs).

There is a well-known saying that three is a crowd, and with Rory in a stable with Westwood and Schwartzel (not to mention the fact that Chubby has always had a great rapport with Westwood) then Rory's decision to leave was no doubt the right one.

The day before he teed off in the WGC Champions event in Shanghai, he said in an interview on the European Tour website:

It's a decision I didn't take lightly. I thought long and hard about it and had a lot of chats with my mum and dad. Sometimes to go forward in your career, you just need to make decisions.

For four years I felt Chubby was the best guy and ISM were fantastic for me but sometimes to progress you need to have a fresh view on things. I feel a new environment around me may enable me to play even better and I feel I'm now moving on to the next stage of my career.

Chubby has been there for me since day one and it was very difficult for me. I remain very close to him – it was purely a business decision and nothing personal at all. I've got all the time in the world for Chubby.

The key line in that statement is where Rory says he feels like wanting 'a new environment around me.' So if he had all the time in the world for Chubby, who had been great to him, who did he want to get away from in that environment, and why?

There is little doubt that apart from his mum and dad, Rory also discussed the situation with his great golfing buddy at the time, Graeme McDowell. McDowell also left Chubby three years previously and went on to win the US Open in 2010. McDowell said:

I've heard that I'm supposed to have enticed Rory – well I purposely took a back seat in it all. Rory makes his own decisions and doesn't listen to anybody. I certainly wasn't going to sway him about what to do with his career. Even if I could, he'd only resent it if it didn't work out.

McDowell also had a few very interesting things to say about the 'reunion' of Westwood and McIlroy, who were paired together in Shanghai a few days after Rory left the team. Westwood's reaction to Rory leaving the team was to say 'It's a bit bizarre.'

In an interview on the 25 October 2011, 'G-Mac' (McDowell) said:

It's very ironic. They'll want to be out beating each other up obviously from a golf point of view. 'Bizarre' is Lee Westwood's opinion but perhaps Rory just wants a different view on things. It's Rory McIlroy's decision and he's a very smart kid.

Rory actually went on to win that inaugural Shanghai Masters event, which was not officially part of the European Tour. It was a new invitation event comprising just 30 players, mainly from Europe and Asia, and four years on it is now the BMW Masters.

After top drawer rounds of 64, 69 and 65 he looked as if he had the massive prize in the bag at -18 under, then almost blew it in the final round with a 72. But it was not over for him yet.

He entered a playoff with American journeyman Anthony Kim. Rory kept his cool to come out on top and collect a whopping cheque for $2 million; the biggest first prize in golf.

Two months after leaving ISM, Rory actually went on to win

again in Asia at the HSBC Hong Kong Open, beating Frenchman Gregory Havret by two strokes on -12. At last he had won his second European Tour, following his Dubai Desert Classic win in 2009.

That victory in early December was welcome relief for Rory on several counts. It was a sort of sweet revenge for losing by two shots to another Frenchman, Gregory Bourdy, in 2009 and also losing there in a Play-Off to Lin Wen-tang in 2008.

It also ended a long run of recent near misses. In reality, some of those near misses were spurned chances; Rory let several of those events slip by and he knew it. A fresh Rory, fully focussed on the job at hand, could have won at least one of them comfortably.

A few months earlier, on 7 September, he finished tied third at the Omega Masters after four brilliant rounds of 65, 69, 67 and 68 for a total of -15. But he just lacked that extra bit of 'oomph', succumbing by five shots to the Dane, Tomas Bjorn, who shot 62.

One week later he really lost it at the KLM Open in Holland with a first round of level par 70 on a fairly easy course. Following that disappointing opening, he finished with a flourish, and rounds of 65, 68 and 67 lifted him to another third place finish with a -10 under total.

At the prestigious Alfred Dunhill Links Championship in Scotland on 5 October, he again shot a poor opening round of 70 but followed it with majestic rounds of 67, 66 and 65 to lose by a single shot to fellow Northern Ireland player Michael Hoey.

The runners-up cheque for €392,000 might have been brilliant consolation for some, but not for Rory. On 9 November at the WGC tournament he also finished fourth and on 30 November he finished fourth in the Omega Mission Hills World Cup.

He was showing great consistency, but without an 'official tour' win, until it finally came in Hong Kong. A magnificent last gasp birdie on the 18th sealed the win for Rory and at the same time lifted him up to world No 2 behind the consistent Luke Donald.

Following this win, Rory's next big moment came in the season-ending Dubai World Championship where he was in with an outside chance of toppling Donald as the new world No 1.

For that to happen, the world No 2 had to win the event, with Donald finishing outside the top nine. But then came drama off the course when he was struck down with a fever – believed to have been caught following his time and travels in Asia.

Test results following his opening 66 showed that his white blood cell count was very low, and he conceded:

The doctor said it could have been 'dengue fever', food poisoning or a number of different things. My immune system is very low and it's taking my body a bit more time to recover than it usually would.

Dengue fever is transmitted by mosquitos but he was assured that the disease, which kills roughly one in 100 people, was only a mild case. On the course, after finding water on the 18th for his second bogey in a row leaving him seven under and five shots off the lead, he added:

To be honest, I'm ready for the season to be done and I'm really looking forward to putting my clubs away.

It was no surprise in the circumstances that things did not get better for Rory. He ended the event in 11th place behind winner Alvaro Quiros. This meant that Luke Donald was crowned winner of the Money Lists on both sides of the Atlantic and was world No 1.

Rory was actually advised to wait in a Dubai hospital for an extra few days and this gave him time to cancel his schedule for Thailand the following week. The media and tabloids had a field day with stories of Rory on a drip in hospital!

With a Christmas of rest and relaxation with his parents and girlfriend, he would be hoping to return fighting fit, fresh and fully charged. In the meantime Rory paid a very nice compliment to Luke Donald on his amazing year and achievements:

I think this week was one too many. But Luke deserves it. Basically every time he's teed it up he's had a chance or he's finished in the top five or ten. Mentally you have to be so tough to keep grinding out the scores when you need to.

It had been one hell of a ride on the rollercoaster in 2011 of 'ups and downs' and 'triumphs and disasters'. But if leaving ISM worked for

McDowell – and he obtained a major out of leaving – then Rory was licking his lips in anticipation of the same.

****

Things did not get any better for Rory when he returned in January of a new year, 2012.

At the Abu Dhabi championship he was pictured with Tiger Woods before the event, smiling and banging drums with the Sheikhs. But the smiles were wiped out on day two.

In a dream team scenario, he played the first couple of days with Tiger Woods and world No 1 Luke Donald and all seemed to be going well for Rory. He began with a five under 67 but then in the second round a bizarre incident happened.

Now, Luke Campbell Donald had recently become winner of the Money Lists on both sides of the Atlantic. He was also the recipient of great praise from Rory at the end of the season, as both fought hard for world No 1 with no let up from either man.

But their friendship and respect could easily have waned next day. At the ninth hole, Rory's second shot ended up six feet off the green just in front of a bunker. There was a little sand from the bunker on the green in Rory's line so he brushed some of it away.

This constituted a breaking of the rules which Rory really should have known. Donald could not believe what he was witnessing; he went over to have words with Rory, which he explained to the waiting reporters afterwards:

I was walking up to my ball and I saw Rory bending down but I was too late. I tried to stop him before he did it and I said 'sorry, I don't think you can do that Rory'. I really had to say something but I wish I'd caught it earlier. Rory thought he was not in the wrong at first so I said 'well, please check and I hope you're right but I think you can only brush loose stuff on the green.'

Tiger Woods was an interested observer as he was the one holding Rory's card in his pocket to mark his scores. The referee intervened and Rory was judged to have broken the rule, for which Tiger then marked him down for a double bogey. Donald added:

A two shot penalty was a bit stiff and maybe one would have been fair. On the next green at the 10th I said sorry to him and I wished I'd caught him earlier but he said not to worry, that it was not my fault. He said it was his mistake for being careless and going brain dead!

That penalty would eventually cost Rory the tournament. He finished the last two days with rounds of 68 and 69 to end 12 under and a shot behind the winner, Robert 'Rocky' Rock of England.

A fortnight later, Rory finished fifth in the Dubai Desert Classic. He looked on course for his second victory in that tournament, opening up with really impressive rounds of 66 and 65, but blew up with final scores of 72 and 71.

Two weeks later, on 26 February, Rory flew to the Arizona desert for the Accenture World Matchplay championships. He first played the event in 2009 where he lost in the quarter final to Geoff Ogilvy (Ogilvy beat Paul Casey to win his second Matchplay title).

Played at Dove Mountain in Marana, Arizona, it is a course built on mountainous desert with plenty of prickly desert scrub lurking for wayward balls off the tee. But Rory likes the layout and loves matchplay from his days as a boys and youth international.

In the event, he had a couple of real tough encounters before he reached the semi-final. There to meet him in a real 'gunfight at the O.K. Corral' was one of the ISM gang – Westy!

It was so ironic that these two should meet here after Rory left ISM the previous year. But make no mistake about it, if there was no needle between them after Westwood's irresistible urge to make comments about Rory, then there was certainly a point to prove.

Graeme McDowell's previous tongue-in-cheek comment that they would want 'to get out there and beat each other up' during a pairing in Shanghai seemed to apply here. Because the truth is, Westwood always felt the need to make comments, which is a no-no.

Prior to the twitter spat, Westwood first riled Rory with his 'it's only an exhibition' comment a few years previously. This was in reference to Rory's pre-Ryder Cup days when he rather immaturely relegated and ranked the Ryder Cup to 'exhibition' status.

Rory later came to put on the record his regret for that remark and he now cherishes the Ryder Cup as one of the top events in golf. But Lee Westwood would not let Rory get away with it and similarly, when asked about Rory leaving ISM, he said, 'it's bizarre'.

Both golfers off-loaded their magazines from the very start. The bullets were flying all over the windy desert and it was clear that each was fully focussed on teaching the other a golf lesson.

Lee Westwood started with a blistering onslaught which Rory had no answer to. He was 3-up through the fourth hole. But Rory composed himself, held his head high and incredibly fought back to lead by the halfway point. He was 1-up through nine holes.

As they came to the 15th Rory was 3-up, but Westwood won the 16th to peg it back to 2-down with just two to play. However, Rory issued the coup-de-grace and won the 17th to win the match 3 and 1 and reach his first World Matchplay final.

It had been a fabulous see-saw battle from both. Inside, McIlroy was no doubt chuffed while Westwood was gutted, and this showed on the 18th. Ryder Cup team mates they may be, but there was no back-slapping, smiles or chat – just a serious handshake and away.

Hunter Mahan of the USA was all that stood between Rory and a first World Matchplay title. It was also the first such final between opponents in their 20s – at the time McIlroy was 22 and Mahan 29.

It could be argued that Mahan had the slightly tougher draw and path to the final. However, he was in a real purple patch and playing some of the best golf of his career. This entire final was typified by what transpired on the very first hole.

Both players missed with their second shot approaches to the green. The American chipped to around 20 feet from the pin but Rory played a superb shot inside Mahan's and to within three feet!

Mahan missed his birdie opportunity and resigned himself to going 1-down after the first hole. Incredibly, McIlroy missed his easy looking birdie putt and they remained all square.

On the par-five third hole both players struck superb third shots to within 10 feet of the hole. Mahan sunk his for birdie and Rory followed him home, so they were still level, then bogeys befell each at the fourth, with Rory finding desert rough and Mahan a bunker.

'The Hunter Gatherer' then went into a different gear. He played scintillating golf and began his surge with a lovely nine iron to within two feet of the hole on the par-three sixth. He went 1-up and was 4-up through 10 holes.

In truth, Rory made too many silly errors which began on the very first hole and plagued him throughout. But he was not helped by Mahan simply teaching him a lesson on the day, the American maintaining the top form he had shown in the previous few days.

Valiantly as Rory tried – and he cut the deficit to 2-down on the 14th hole after a great pitch to within eight feet – it was Hunter Mahan's day. He let the holes run out until there was no way back for Rory and he triumphed on a 2 and 1 score.

It was Mahan's first victory since his 2010 win at the prestigious Bridgestone Invitational and his fourth in all following previous wins at the Travellers Championship (2007) and Phoenix Open (2010). He lifted the trophy and clutched a cheque for €1,061,000.

A few months later, in April, Mahan would add the Shell Houston Open to his impressive resume (he further added The Barclays in 2014 for No 6). The Houston win lifted him to an all-time high ranking of world No 4 and the highest American in the rankings.

So McIlroy did not lose to any old slouch. Mahan is sheer class. After collecting his own handsome runner-up prize of €644,000, Rory referred to a poor front nine with three bogeys, a double bogey and the missed short putt to win the opening hole. He surmised:

I just left myself too much to do. It wasn't to be but I didn't have my best game with me this week.

Mahan was very magnanimous in victory. He was also extremely honest about his inner deepest feelings as he drove off on the first tee. In the same breath however, he did show great sportsmanship as he offered these words in tribute to Rory:

Deep down I wanted to postpone that crowning of number one player in the world for Rory. He'll get there. He's phenomenal. He's really talented. He'll be number one eventually.

Chapter 2

IRISH GOLF'S FIRST
WORLD NUMBER ONE

After losing in the final of the World Matchplay to Hunter Mahan, Rory McIlroy was far from downbeat. He took it all on the chin and it was as if the trip to the deserts of Arizona was an excursion and a bonus, away from tournament golf.

Matchplay brings Rory back to his days as an amateur when he played Boys and Youths inter-provincial matches as well as representing Ireland in Internationals. He thrives on it and it is probably a welcome break from constantly trying to shoot low scores.

In talking to the media after his loss, he said:

I'm happy with how I'm playing and hopefully it won't be long before I'm winning again. I've got two more tournaments before the Masters and that's what I'm really building up to.

At the beginning of every season Rory will always have his sights firmly fixed on just one golf tournament – the US Masters at Augusta, Georgia. Everything prior to that is geared towards getting himself into prime and peak form for that event.

That does not mean other tournaments are unimportant. Nothing could be further from the truth. Most events carry points for the world rankings and so they are food for Rory's big quest for world No 1.

In recent years, the hugely important Fedex Cup has also come along, but the Masters and its 'Green Jacket' is the major that Rory craves most. He actually explained this in an interview before the Wells Fargo championship in Charlotte, Carolina, in early May 2012:

I don't want to be burned out by the time I'm 30. I want to try and prolong my career as much as possible. I sometimes take a little bit too much out of myself, especially at the end of a season. [I referred earlier to his season end in 2011 when he was hospitalised].

Basically, the most important time for me is from the start of April until the end of August. That's when all the big tournaments are and when you want to play your best golf. All the stuff either side of that is more preparation work and making sure your game is getting ready and your body is physically ready for that time of the year. I know I've been criticised a little bit for not playing as much as some other guys leading into those weeks but that's because I know I've a big stretch ahead of me and I want to be as fresh as possible.

The first of those two events before the Masters arrived a week later, on 4 March.Rory teed off in the first round of the Honda Classic at Palm Beach in Florida. After an unremarkable first round at four under, 66, he was barely audible in the media tent, saying 'I'm going to go to the gym after I've had a bit of lunch here.'

Journalists did not know whether he was dejected or fatigued after a round which, by his lofty standards, was very poor. He hit only 12 of 18 greens in regulation; found eight of 14 fairways; had five birdies and one bogey and yet he was still a very healthy four under par.

However, he did hint at fatigue as he added 'I might take a little bit of a nap and catch up on some sleep as I've been up since 5.15 this morning.'

Things did not get any better for Rory the following day when he shot 67. But after shooting another 66 in the penultimate round, joint best of the day, he suddenly found himself in the lead going into the final round without setting the world alight.

In fact, the first three days had been rather dull and drab for one of the highest quality fields of the season assembled. The best was saved until last when fireworks flooded the final round. The chief pyromaniac in the field being Tiger Woods!

Woods was having one of those events where it looked likely that, after just making the cut, his effort would take its toll with a finish somewhere down the field. That looked to be the way things were going when he was nine shots adrift of Rory going into the final day.

But the greens and fairways suffered scorched earth from the hand of Tiger that day and the crowd went wild. As Rory teed up, and up until the midpoint of his round, he knew from the hollering and whooping of the crowds that Tiger was in the zone.

Soon he would see Tiger prowling up behind him on the leaderboard as Woods had hit three birdies and an eagle coming to his 17th and penultimate hole. If he could birdie the final two holes then he would put Rory and the leaders under a good degree of pressure.

Tiger birdied the 17th and was six under for his round. When that putt rolled in and Tiger, in his own inimitable way, walked spritely after it with that killer look of his, Rory had to contain the fact that the crowd, the media and almost everyone wanted Tiger to win.

He was now the people's champion after being in the wars the previous few years, usurped in the world rankings by Luke Donald and Rory. There was talk that Tiger was finished. That he would never be the same again. This round disproved all that.

Rory was on the 12th and had not done anything of note in his round. Tiger was within three shots of his lead, having been nine behind overnight. It is one thing trying to play percentage golf to contain your lead, it is quite another to deal with a rampaging Tiger.

Incredibly, he eagled the 18th! The explosion of noise all over the course must have rocked Rory off his feet. Tiger, from nowhere, had shot 62 in a round that included two eagles. He was just a shot behind McIlroy. It was his lowest final round score in 17 years.

The way he played that final hole was a flashback to the genius and Woods of old. A perfect drive was followed by a five iron from 216 yards over water guarding the green. His ball came to rest eight feet away, stone dead and job done after a great day at the office.

Woods freshened up after signing his cards and went to watch the television. He had one eye on the Dodgers ball game and the other on how Rory and those up front were playing. More importantly: how they would respond and react to his gallant efforts.

At the time of his magnificent eagle, young Rory was on the 13th green lining up an eight-foot birdie putt of his own that would move him two shots ahead of Tiger. McIlroy nailed it and made pars the rest of the way home for a two shot win and the coveted top ranking.

He was world No 1 at last after trying so hard for so long for the win that would leap him over Luke Donald. It was richly deserved. He had shown real 'champion' qualities and this Honda Classic was one of the most important wins in his career, for a variety of reasons.

More pertinently, the victory can be seen as a turning point. In holding Woods at bay, it really signaled a changing of the guard. Tiger had his glory in his prime as a young man and this is a young man's game. Rory was tops.

However, more than anything else, this win really showed that Rory now knew how to hold a lead and how, after his Masters collapse, he would not panic. When he birdied on the 13th for a two shot lead, he knew that with a par five to finish he just had to play sensibly.

Rory referred to this in his media briefing afterwards. He talked about the noise all over the course and how he could not ignore it. But he said that he knew if he rolled the birdie putt in on the 13th that he was virtually home and hosed.

A champagne moment as he was now making news all across the globe as golf's new number one player. Luke Donald immediately tweeted him a message of congratulations which read: 'Congratulations. Enjoy the view!'

The response from Rory in tweets, newspapers and with friends was always the same: he stated that 'it might only be for 15 minutes'; 'it won't last long' and that he was only 'keeping the position warm' for Luke.

Nevertheless, it was a monumental moment. World No 1 status is a feat that only the true greats of the game achieve. This is one area that there can never be anything lucky or fluky about it. It is earned through hard work, skill and, above all, consistency.

Since the USPGA in August 2011, he played in 11 ranking events and finished outside the top five in only one of them. That was the sort of top drawer form that won him this coveted accolade. When asked what it meant to him he replied:

It means an awful lot to be able to call yourself the No 1 player in the world; it is a great achievement. I am very honoured to join the list of guys who have held that spot. Hopefully I can keep a hold it for a little while.

Rory McIlroy also became the first golfer from the island of Ireland to achieve world No 1 status.

In downplaying somewhat the length of time he would remain as world No 1, it was as if Rory could sense that Luke Donald was still playing his best golf and that he would be around for a while yet and challenging him at every corner for the position.

If that was the case then he was so right. Donald had become the best player in the world in May 2011 when he won the BMW PGA Championship at Wentworth in England. He had held it for almost a year – 40 weeks to be exact – until Rory won that Honda Classic.

But he would become world No 1 again soon. In fact, between the pair of them, they would exchange top honours on no less than four occasions throughout that season. In the meantime, McIlroy further stretched his world rankings lead the following week.

Traveling a relatively short distance from Palm Beach to Doral to contest the WGC Cadillac event, Rory narrowly missed out on a second successive victory. A poor first round 73 was a spoiler before rounds of 69, 65 and 67 lifted him to third place.

Another very consistent top five finish, and the perfect form and results from those two tournaments in advance of his 'holy grail' – the US Masters. He was now in better shape than the previous season when he won the US Open as he was improving hand over fist.

He was also officially the best player on the planet and his decision to leave ISM was, if not vindicated, then certainly a move in the right direction towards peace of mind and reaching his true potential.

The rankings after his Honda win read: McIlroy 9.30, Donald 8.97 and Westwood 8.19 but he now increased that lead to almost a full point on 9.85. However, on 18 March and fully two weeks after Rory hit top spot, Luke Donald leapt back to the top!

Donald won the Transitions Championship in the States to become the first of the two to hit a perfect ten with a rankings score of 10.03. Humorously, Rory immediately tweeted: 'Well, I enjoyed it while it lasted! Congrats @Luke Donald. Impressive performance.'

By this time Rory was now under new management. He had joined up with fellow Irish players Graeme McDowell and Shane Lowry under the umbrella of the Dublin based Horizon Sports Management company, run by Conor Ridge.

Both Ridge and McIlroy soon took up a very special invitation to meet Barack Obama, the President of the United States, just a few days before St Patrick's Day. Like a scene from the film 'Reservoir Dogs', they both looked dapper in black suits and ties.

At the plush dinner Rory was also introduced to British Prime Minister David Cameron, but as Obama is a very keen golfer himself, both Rory and Barack were seen in deep demonstrative conversation.

It transpired that the President informed Rory that he was not happy with his own golf swing. He sought out some tips from Rory who, talking about the experience, tweeted the President next day: 'Unbelievable experience at the White House last night! Big thanks to @BarackObama for the invite! We'll get that golf swing sorted soon!'

When the President visited Ireland on 17 June the following year for a summit of world leaders in Enniskillen, he mentioned his meeting with Rory in the White House saying: 'I met Rory last year and he offered to get my swing sorted.'

On hearing of Obama's remark, Rory later tweeted: 'Nice of @BarackObama to mention me in his speech in Belfast today.'

It is a fact that 15 of the last 18 US Presidents played golf. The exceptions were Herbert Hoover, Harry Truman and Jimmy Carter. Dwight Eisenhower could not get enough of it. He had a putting green installed close to the Oval Office!

Barrack Obama took up golf as a teenager when he lived for a while in Hawaii. He remains tight-lipped concerning his golf game but rumour has it that he is somewhere around the 17 handicap mark.

The word is that he is desperately trying to get that mark down and has been criticised in some quarters for playing too much golf. It is not always possible but, weather permitting, he tries to get in one round of golf a week.

In fact, President Obama played his 200th round of golf on October 12th 2014 when he got in a Sunday morning game at Fort Belvoir Golf Club in Alexandria, Virginia. But he has some rounds to go before getting anywhere near two former 'Commander-in-Chiefs'.

President Woodrow Wilson is documented as having played 1,600 rounds of golf and Dwight Eisenhower played around half that –

800. Eisenhower was such a fanatical golfer that he was a member of Augusta National.

Fittingly, after Washington, Rory's next golfing port of call a fortnight later was 2604 Washington Road in Atlanta, Georgia, and a drive up through the splendour of Magnolia Drive to Augusta National. It was all systems go for the US Masters.

But as Rory prepared to be driven up there for the 2012 event, there is little doubt that his heart would be pumping fast. He would be a bundle of nerves as he recalled memories from an unbelievable, unforgettable and ultimately forgettable tournament in 2011.

Almost exactly a year before, as Rory was driven through there, he was leaving with his tail between his legs after one of the most infamous collapses in US Master's history. The whole episode gave rise to a well-known euphemism: 'Rory's Masters Meltdown'.

Chapter 3

AUGUSTA – A SOBERING RETURN

When Rory McIlroy returned to the scene of his infamous collapse at Augusta the previous year – now euphemistically known as 'Rory's Masters Meltdown' – he was quite engaging, relaxed and full of fun at the pre-Masters press conference.

The nightmarish memories of squandering a four shot lead and shooting 80, which included a triple bogey at the 10th, seemed to have been put firmly in the past. He also revealed that earlier, he had ventured out on the course to take a look at that 10th hole.

Rory revisited the exact location where his ball came to rest between cabins in 2011. His drive ricocheted from a tree branch and came to rest in woods between cabins. In living memory, no golfer had ever ended up in there before. An incredulous McIlroy said: 'I can't believe [now] how far off the tee the cabins are. They must be only 50 yards away.'

Rory also revealed that he had received a very generous, heart warming and inspiring phone call from Greg Norman. The Australian suffered a fate similar to Rory when he lost a huge final round lead to Nick Faldo.

Having not played competitively since the Cadillac event almost three weeks before, the comments about his lengthy breaks were doing the rounds again from fellow pros. One player to offer his opinion on the matter was none other than Lee Westwood.

When asked what he thought about Rory going into the Masters after a three week break, he said: 'I'd much rather be going into the Masters having not played for three days competitively than for three weeks.'

Granted it is an unusually long period for a golfer to take off before a major. Using the British Open as an example, most professionals will play the Scottish Open or a US Tour event the week before, or even practise a few rounds on a links in the UK or Ireland.

McIlroy countered this argument by saying that if you look at his record between breaks then you will see a pattern emerge. Before the break he was playing for many weeks and after returning, he would be a far fresher player and would get better by the round.

Just as the session was about to end, his phone rang out its ring tone. Rory quickly silenced it and said, 'Oops, no phone calls [mobile phones] at Augusta!' A member of Augusta sitting next to him replied, 'We'll just pretend we didn't hear it.'

At 1.42 pm on Thursday, Rory teed off in the company of Bubba Watson and one Angel Cabrera. Now if Rory was trying to banish all thoughts of events the previous year, then Cabrera was not the man to have beside him.

The big Argentine, who could easily fit two Rorys into his bulky frame, was the man who was birdying holes as if shelling peas during Rory's meltdown. But McIlroy steadied the ship in this first round and without doing anything spectacular finished one under, at 71.

That left him just inside the top 20 and four shots adrift of overnight leader Lee Westwood. The next day McIlroy outshone both of his huge hitting partners to post a -3, 69, and climb to a shot behind joint leaders Fred Couples and Jason Duffner. Then disaster struck.

Paired with Sergio Garcia in the penultimate round, they both had a day to forget. Rory had three sixes in his first nine holes for a score of 42. Garcia shot 40. Things improved a little turning for home but not by much. The par three 12th summed up their miserable day.

Golden Bell is one of the shortest par-three holes in golf majors. But it can also prove tricky and treacherous with 'Raes Creek' in front, swirling winds and bunkers. But both Sergio and Rory nailed their shots to the green for possible birdies.

They both three-putted for bogey! As they walked off the green, they turned, caught each others sniggering faces and decided to stage a mock hug and embrace. They laughed all the way to the 13th and all the way home. As Rory explained after:

*If you can't laugh at yourself, who can you laugh at? It seems like
every year I come out here, I throw in a bad nine holes out there.
It was good to have Sergio at my side today even if we didn't have
great days.*

Rory's fourth US Masters appearance effectively ended after a +5,
77. Things did not improve much next day. In his final round he
shot a +4, 76 and ended the event in a share of 40th place as Bubba
Watson won, beating Louis Oosthuizen in an astonishing playoff.

Standing by his principles, Rory took another month off tour before
reappearing at the Wells Fargo event on 6 May. It is important here
to recall Rory's very own reasoning for taking such lengthy periods
away from golf.

Before his return to Augusta, he said that taking such time off
was necessary for him so that he would come back 'refocused and
refreshed'. That seemed to work for the first half of the Masters, when
he found himself just a shot behind the leaders until he blew up.

Behind the scenes, what most people fail to realise is that
professional golfers take large periods of time off in order to work on
their game. This is especially the case if a player has had a bad time
in his previous tournament, which is what befell Rory in Augusta.

Time off allows a player to spend hours and days working on
aspects of his or her game, such as driving, swing, posture, putting
and all sorts of other areas. 'Hard practise' is something that the
greats like Gary Player and Jack Nicklaus strongly advocate.

However there was a big price to pay for Rory's absence.
Following his miserable Masters, Luke Donald finished third in the
Zurich Classic at the end of April and so reclaimed the world No 1
spot, having lost it briefly two weeks previously.

Quail Hollow for the Wells Fargo championship is one of Rory's
favourite events. It was there in 2010 that he not only won his first
'biggie' on the US Tour, but he also tore the course apart with a
course record round of -10, 62.

On the eve of his 23rd birthday, he opened up with a -2, 70 and
next day the birthday boy improved better still in his second round.
Starting on the 10th, he birdied that as well as the 11th and 15th before
giving one back on the 18th.

He rallied again with further birdies on the fifth and ninth to finish with a -4, 68 for the day and six under for the tournament. He was nicely poised in 13th place at the half way point and was reasonably happy, stating:

I have been able to get it around and being six under after two rounds is pretty good considering the way I've hit the ball. I just need to do some work this afternoon on the range and hopefully play better on the weekend. To be honest, a lot of my drives are ending up in the semi rough. You do need to hit the fairways here to give yourself every chance but I'll take 68.

'Moving Day' saw Rory do just that. He shot a superb -6, 66 to be -12 for the tournament and two shots behind joint leaders Webb Simpson and Ryan Moore. He would go out in the penultimate group and with a chance of winning his second Wells Fargo in three years.

All the drama happened on the last couple of holes. Rory was three under for his round coming to the 17th hole and he was in a share of the lead at 15 under with 35 year old 'journeyman' D .A Points.

Rory dropped a shot at that hole to fall a shot behind Points who made par. It looked like he would fall short again as the title was Points' to lose. The little known American was playing out of his skin and had not dropped a shot for his past 39 holes!

Talk about pressure; talk about nerves and bottle and then there is the cruel hand of fate. Why oh why did it take Points until the very last hole to drop a shot, as he did on the 18th? Destiny has dealt this sinister card on countless numerous occasions.

There was a look of horror and abject disappointment on his face as he stooped to pick his bogey ball from the hole. It was his first dropped shot in 40 holes and the look on his face was also one of resignation. He was resigned to the fact that Rory looked victorious.

As Points stood back watching, another dramatic moment was to follow. Rory stood over a 15-foot putt for the title. Photographers got into position, fully expecting to snap more glory for worldwide media exposure. He missed!

The two men shook hands knowing they would have to go to a

playoff. Another man who was watching the drama unfold from the clubhouse would join them. Clad in his now-famous orange boiler-suit, Oklahoma's own Rickie Fowler also finished 14 under.

Back to the 18th tee they trawled in their buggies with caddies and clubs in tow. Smiles, sips of water, handshakes and the hearts were thumping again. Without any doubt, the trio held various emotions in their bodies.

It is certain that at least one body was ravaged by nervous tension to the point that he could hear his heart in his ears as he unleashed his drive. His legs also felt weak. Another surely felt calm with nothing to lose and with a sense of 'gung ho' and 'give-it-a-go'.

No doubt one of them also had the feeling that he was destined to win, because he was playing like he had not played in a long time. He was playing magnificently. Every shot he played was sublime. As Tiger would say, 'he had his A-game with him'.

McIlroy left the other two in his wake. His drive measured an astonishing 340 yards. He was in pole position. But Fowler was not too far behind and Points, who was trying to battle the demons of what had befallen him a few minutes before, still held every chance.

We would not have to wait long for the outcome. There would be no second tie hole to negotiate. The matter was settled with their second shots to the green. Rory and D .A hit fairly tame efforts while Ricky Fowler played the shot of his life. The shot of his career.

He played his second shot before Rory and the result, with the crowds going wild, was probably the reason why Rory followed with a poor effort, because Rory now had that feeling of resignation knowing that he would need something amazing to better Fowler's.

Ricky's shot came to rest four feet from the pin. A few minutes later, he duly slotted home for his first Tour win. How ironic that two young men tipped and touted to dominate world golf into the future had both won their maiden US titles at Quail Hollow.

It is also worth noting that Ricky Fowler is two years younger than Rory and both played in the 2007 Walker Cup. Some consolation for Rory lay in the fact that in his see-saw battle with Donald for world No 1, he had just leapfrogged back to the top again.

Ever the sportsman, McIlroy paid a generous compliment to his good friend Fowler:

You wouldn't call the 18th today a birdie hole with the pin situated where it was. So for Rickie to go out and play that hole the way he did, he deserved to win.

In total contrast to his beloved Wells Fargo event, the Players Championship is without doubt an event that Rory travels to with a feeling of apprehension. 'Sawgrass' is a course which, to date, he has not really taken to.

Every golfer on the planet, amateur or professional, comes across a golf course (or hole) where at the first instant he or she sees it, a dislike or discomfort is formed. When that happens it is very hard to eradicate the feeling and it will continue to persist.

Rory no doubt heard about the so-called fifth major when he was growing up. He heard about its infamous 17th hole and he probably watched down through the years a lot of the carnage that unfolded at that hole.

The following is an excerpt from the previous book, 'Rory – His Story So Far'. It gives you a feeling of Rory's thoughts concerning the 'Players' before he ever played it and how he has played it since:

"Over the years, Rory no doubt watched from his armchair, amid much amusement like the rest of us, as great golfers found themselves in big trouble there. No hole better illustrates the treacherous condition of Sawgrass than its infamous 17th.

Requiring no more than a wedge, this short par-three still manages year after year to make fools out of the world's greatest golfers. The reason – from the tee, the green looks like a tiny target set against the backdrop of it being surrounded on all sides by water.

It is a cruel hole. Each year as the 160 golfers begin their rounds here, almost every single one of them has the 17th on their minds. As they play through the previous holes, they are all acutely aware of that 'bogey hole' lying in wait up ahead.

During the course of their rounds, golfers can hear the roars, the screams, the shrieks and the 'oooohs and ahhhhs' of the crowds which signals to them that another ball has hit the water.

Then, when their own time has come to stand on that 17th, with spectators and millions watching on TV, it can be akin to standing in front of a judge in court, or worse still, an executioner. The pressure can be enormous with many legs and limbs turning to jelly.

Here is another interesting take on Sawgrass and on Rory McIlroy which was written by Jay Busbee. Born Howard James Busbee Jr., he is an American novelist, sportswriter, comic book writer and well known golf bloggist. He wrote:

These kids today and their video games. So locked into their Xboxes and their Wiis and their Playstation 3s, they don't know what to do with life when it smacks 'em right in the face.

Case in point: Rory McIlroy, who knows a thing or two about both real golf and the video kind. He kills time between tournaments by playing 'Tiger Woods '09', and just this week got his first live taste of Sawgrass, a course he's completely mastered - he once shot a 54 over 18 virtual holes - on the game.

Rory's verdict, according to Reuters:

It's a lot different. You get up to holes like 11 on the computer and you can drive it up to the big tree on the right, which is like 150 from the green, I had a good drive yesterday and was still hitting a five wood in, it is not quite like it is on the Play Station.

Yeah, I've found that hunting zombies and carjacking a Ferrari in South Beach is a lot tougher in real life than it is in video games, too (Tip: neither one is recommended). Now, unlike the rest of us, McIlroy can actually play as himself in the game without having to create a slightly more muscular, slightly more handsome version of ourselves. Even so, no matter how graphically accurate the simulation may be, he's not even close to experiencing the real thing - not unless he's got a constant loop of goofballs yelling 'Get in the hole!' running on his iPod as he plays.'

To many, it is euphemistically referred to as 'The Island Green'. Rory was to get his very first taste of it and it would not be pleasant on his palate. He was not spared or shown any mercy.

Even though he was -2, he really struggled through his round which included three bogeys. Then splash! Rory took a triple-bogey six at the 137-yard beast! Karl MacGinty of the Irish Independent described Rory's tee shot:

The Holywood youngster's jaw dropped in astonishment after his tee shot, hit with a wedge, flew right over the island green and disappeared into the dark green water. McIlroy turned and looked at his caddie, JP Fitzgerald, in disbelief. 'Did you ever see a wedge fly 150 yards,' he was still asking as he left the recorder's hut after signing for a first round 74.

This is what Rory felt about his first ever dice with the dreaded 17th of Sawgrass:

It was 148 yards to the pin today. I hit a wedge and just flew the lot. I don't know if I got a gust or something. I wasn't going big with my third shot from the drop zone. I spun it back to the front and took three to get down.

Rory was two under coming to that 17th hole. Less than half an hour later, he finished his round +2. The next day, Rory missed the cut. This time he got through it unscathed but the rest of his round was not so good.

He signed for a +5, 77 in a round that included 5 bogeys and a double bogey seven at the par-five 9th hole. The course had left a bitter taste in Rory's mouth. Without any question, it was the dreaded 17th which caused all the problems to begin with and sent Rory home.'

Things did not get any better in 2012 as Rory missed a second succesive cut at the Players Championship. He may have mastered it in its 'virtual' format on screen, but the 'live' fresh air version is something that Rory continues to struggle with.

Chapter 4

MADE IN THE USPGA

The missed cut at the 2012 Players Championship followed on from Rory popping back across the Atlantic to play the BMW at Wentworth, where he also missed the cut with rounds of 74 and 79.

It set in motion a miserable sequence of events and 'M/C's. Three weeks after Sawgrass, he missed another cut on the US Tour before finishing seventh in the St Jude Classic. He may have been buoyed by that but it was only a temporary respite, as worse was to follow.

Rory teed off at the Olympic Club in San Francisco on 14 June in defence of his US Open crown in a very good frame of mind thanks to St Jude. But it was to be a lost cause. He was all at sea in a first round horror 77.

He improved marginally the next day by shooting 73 but it was too little, too late. Rory would not be defending his crown over the weekend. For a holder of a major, that was somewhat embarrassing. Defending champions do their utmost to play the full event.

Two weeks later, girlfriend Caroline Wozniacki joined Rory for the Irish Open. Amid all the frustration, Rory's smiles shone again with the help and urgings of a partisan home crowd.

Rounds of 70, 69 qualified him for the weekend and although he hit a disappointing 71 on moving day, a magnificent -5, 67 on Sunday shot him up to a tie for 10th place. It was just the tonic he needed for the British Open, three weeks later.

Another great fillip was the addition of Michael Bannon to Rory's team. Bannon had coached Rory since he was a boy but was now only occasionally helping out. But an SOS had been sent out to Bannon.

A full time golf teacher and coach in Bangor, Northern Ireland, he left that position to join McIlroy on tour as his new full time coach. Both were caught on BBC television cameras at the Open. The pair worked on various aspects of Rory's swing.

His game looked like it was in need of a lot of work as he finished way down the field with the also-rans and, if seasons are measured in terms of majors (which Rory's are), then this one scored 'woeful'.

Tied 40th in the Masters, M/C in the US Open and tied 60th in the British Open was just not good enough for a player tipped to be one of the all-time greats of golf. He had one chance left in the USPGA. Whatever issues Rory had, they had to be sorted – and fast.

The Bridgestone Invitational two weeks later was the last event before the USPGA the following week. It looked like he was struggling again after an even-par round of 70 to start. But rounds of 67, 67 and 68 meant he finished in a tie for fifth without threatening.

It was promising; so much so that London's 'Racing Post' newspaper picked Rory as one of their selections to win the final major of the year. They touted his hitting the ball 344 yards at the Bridgestone, adding that if his putting was better, he would have won.

That aside, a pattern was emerging. Some terrible performances were followed by a Top 10 finish but he could not seem to string two good results together. Then the USPGA arrived, an event for which he did have an excellent record.

In three previous attempts at the USPGA, Rory was actually in with a great chance of winning. His debut at Hazeltine GC, Minnesota, in 2009 saw near record crowds turn up to watch the 91st running of what is traditionally the season-ending major.

Tiger Woods opened up with a -5, 67 in the first round to lead by one shot from Padraig Harrington. Rory shot a -1, 71 and he was quite content with his very first performance in the event, especially since Hazeltine is a tough course.

A second round of +1, 73 left him well off the pace as Woods increased his lead at the top to seven under, but another round of 71 on the third day put him back into under par figures for the tournament and he was not out of it.

He shot another nice round on the final day. But a -2, 70 was never going to trouble Tiger Woods and Y E Yang, and Rory finished his first USPGA at three under in a tie for third place with Lee Westwood.

Woods, who led going into the final round and seemed sure to add yet another major to his haul, buckled under the pressure of Yang's dogged persistence. The Korean matched him shot for shot and eventually won by three shots on eight under par.

Yang became the first Asian to win the USPGA but it was a case of what might have been for another Irishman. Behind Tiger Woods going into that final round, Padraig Harrington actually started the day level with Yang.

However, when he looks back on this particular event, he will wish to forget in a hurry the horror that befell him on a fairly easy par three. Padraig blew his chances of winning a fourth major by running up a 'quintuple-bogey' eight on that eighth hole!

Rory admitted to showing very poor judgement on the greens. He started with a double-bogey but then hit a rich vein of form by rattling in four birdies. Another bogey on the 12th, and some missed opportunities, put paid to his chance of victory.

Nevertheless, it was his highest finish in a major to date and summing up, he said:

I've had some good results lately and I'm looking to build on these results next year and hopefully try to do a bit better. I think coming into this week, I didn't have my best form or my best game with me. So to finish tied third is a great result for me.

Onto 2010 at Whistling Straits, and Rory would come even closer to winning the USPGA. He did indeed build on his impressive debut from the previous year and by the time he left Whistling Straits, he could only think of how close he came to victory.

Similar to Hazeltine the previous year, he opened with a pretty ordinary 71. He followed that with a -4, 68 in the second round to lie on five under par at the halfway mark. It was also a case of two cuts made from two in the USPGA.

Leader Matt Kuchar on eight under par led by a shot from Nick Watney so Rory was in a nice position with two days to go. Watney, though, had other ideas. On 'moving day', he put space between himself and the rest of the field by shooting a magnificent 66 to go to -13.

Not to be outdone, and keeping himself very much in the hunt,

Rory shot 67 and was only three shots back on -10. He was level with Dustin Johnson and both would play in the second-to-last pairing on the final day.

Alas, and for the second year running, things just did not swing Rory's way. Although he got the better of Watney, who fell apart with a final round 81, Bubba Watson shot a final round 68 to join Martin Kaymer in a playoff at -11.

Agonisingly, Rory had finished just a single shot adrift. Although he had tied third yet again, it was hard for him to stomach the fact that he had failed to break par in the last round. Had he managed to do so, he would have gone close to winning. He said:

I'm ok. I had a few bad swings the first few holes and I managed to recover well. After those escapes, I had a few chances that went by on the back nine. It was just one of those days when I felt I hit good putts but nothing went in. I'm pleased overall as I played nicely all week and I just needed to find one more shot in there on any of the four days, which is disappointing.

I was very proud at how I ground it out. It wasn't the start that I would have wanted. I made a great up and down at the first hole and another great up and down at the third and I held it together on the front nine.

There was however one worrying aspect concerning something else he said. In light of what would eventually happen to him in the last round of his 'Masters Meltdown', it was very significant that he admitted to feeling the heat as he went out for the final round:

It was my first time being in contention in the last round of a major and in the second-to-last group. I was feeling it on the first tee and it was a new experience for me. Hopefully it will stand me in good stead for the future.

Tying third in his first two USPGA's, one could see the reasons why Rory now fancied himself to win it in future. He stated as such before the 2011 event but the drama that would unfold there was something that no-one, least of all Rory, could see coming.

Going into the event at the Atlanta Athletic Club course, he must have been quietly confident. The omens also looked good when he was paired with fellow countryman Darren Clarke. Very quickly, it turned into an event full of controversy.

On the third hole, Rory hit his tee shot into the semi rough. But unknown to him, to the television crews and to the watching millions, an amazing thing happened. A small boy walked over to his ball and picked it up!

Before Rory arrived on the scene, the child's parents told the toddler to put it back where he had found it. The drama was only beginning. The young child placed the ball at the foot of a tree.

Although the ball was in a very tricky position nestled directly behind a tree, Rory saw no great cause for alarm. Like almost every golfer on the planet who has at some stage encountered this scenario – amateur and professional – he knew he had a few options.

Normally it boils down to two – have a good firm go at it or take the safe choice and play it out gently onto the fairway. There is a third – taking a penalty drop – but Rory, after surveying the ball, and feeling it was sitting up nicely, decided to have a go.

After giving the ball a good strong strike, it ricocheted up into the air and came to rest just a few feet away with his club flying through the air. The latter was actually part of the plan as he later explained:

It was dangerous. I thought if I could make contact with the ball and just let the club go, I might get away with it. It was a shot that I felt like, if I took it on and pulled it off, it could have saved me a shot.

Grasping his wrist in pain however, it soon became clear that something bad had happened. Just underneath the ball, and invisible to the eye, was the root of a tree. Any gardener will testify that it must have been like striking hard rock or stone.

Rory immediately called for ice and was also given the option of a ten minute time-out, which he refused. Returning to his ball, which was now a little way back from the tree, he decided this time to hit out and put bend on the ball.

He played it very well leaving an up-and-down for bogey. Furthermore, and after his second shot from behind the tree, there seemed to be no adverse effect from his injury, and so he carried on with an ice-pack wrapped around his wrist and forearm.

A discussion with officials about getting his club repaired showed that he was almost certainly going to complete his round. But there was more cause for worry, as on the follow through from his tee shot on the fourth hole he winced in pain.

But again he soldiered on. So much so that the crowd warmed to him on the fifth as he chatted with Darren Clarke. Grimacing again after his tee shot there, the crowd shouted, "'hang in there Rory'", to which he replied several times, "thank you".

It was also quite noticeable that he had no strength in his right hand because of the pain in his arm. When bending down to stick his tee in the ground, he winced in pain and had to put the tee into his left hand to shove it into the ground.

Through all his trials and tribulations, his talent and genius was about to shine through once more. He splashed out of a bunker to within a foot for a tap-in birdie and he made it consecutive birdies on the sixth.

Comparisons were being made with Tiger Woods who famously won a major on one leg! The golf media were quickly latching on to the fact that Rory had gone from one over to one under on one arm!

And so his dramatic day continued. His fascinating and intriguing round was followed by bogeys and birdies and a physio accompanied Rory for a few holes before deeming him fit to continue. He ended with a par 70 which was a fantastic effort in the circumstances.

Rory was seemingly ok to continue his USPGA but reflecting back on his opening round, and particularly that third hole, he admitted: 'It was a mistake in judgment'.

After entering the Atlanta Athletic Club clubhouse for a few minutes, he brought out some extra wet towels from the locker room. He then got into the back seat of his courtesy car, driven by friend and associate Stuart Cage, and it was off to the doctors.

An MRI scan late on Thursday night showed no long term damage. A strained tendon in his right wrist was diagnosed and, to great applause, Rory appeared on the tee on Friday morning. Before that, he said:

If it wasn't a major, I probably would have stopped yesterday. To be honest, looking at the scans, they said, 'Look, you can't do any more damage to it, it's up to yourself. If you want to play and you feel as though you can play ok and carry on, then do. And if not, then you shouldn't play.' I feel as if I can play, so the decision was purely up to me.

With his wrist heavily strapped, and a new seven-iron from Titleist to replace the one that was broken in the battle with the root the previous day, Rory went out and shot a +3, 73.

All things considered, and with so many big names missing the cut, he did very well to make the weekend. It was three out of three cuts made in USPGA's. Even then, he was not at all happy – and it had nothing to do with his wrist but everything to do with the 17th hole in his second round.

On the 16th, he swung in a fantastic birdie from nearly 50 feet to get to one under par for the tournament. The crowds went wild hollering and yelling out his name as he headed to the 207-yard par three over water.

With his new seven-iron in hand approaching the tee, he then changed his mind and switched to a six-iron. Looking at it anxiously in mid-air, he seemed to hit it a bit higher than he wanted.

He was shocked when it came down short of the green, and glancing over at caddie J P Fitzgerald, he muttered inquisitively 'Wet?' Worse was to follow as he three-putted for a triple bogey which killed off all his momentum. His 2011 USPGA was over.

Another 'Irishman' actually won that 2011 USPGA, and in the process also won his first major. Keegan Bradley was a most unlikely winner of the event. He and the rest of the field looked to be playing second fiddle to Jason Dufner.

Duffner, who had failed to win on the US Tour in his seven years playing it, was out on his own. With just four holes left in his round, he led by five shots. His first win looked assured. His first success was also set to become his first major win.

But even worse than McIlroy's Masters debacle – the young Rory had a full round in front of him – the experienced Dufner suffered a most amazing collapse. In sight of the chequered flag, he threw it all away.

Bradley himself looked to have blown his chances when he triple bogeyed the par-three 15th. However, he showed steely resolve to brilliantly birdie both 16 and 17 to go into a three-hole playoff with Dufner.

Indeed, when the crowd burst into their Olympic-like chant of 'USA, USA, USA' to signal the fact that America were about to end their majors drought, it seemed to give Dufner even more of the wobbles whilst at the same time inspiring Bradley.

As the playoff ended, and Bradley threw his arms in the air to celebrate victory, little did he know that he had just etched himself into history as the first golfer to win a major with a long putter. The 25 year old admitted afterwards:

When I was 12 I did a bit of skiing. I was competing in a slalom in Killington. I remember sitting on the top of that hill. It was raining, cold, sleeting and I remember thinking to myself 'I love golf so much more'. But this is unbelievable because two and a half years ago, I was on the Hooters Tour grinding for survival.

Thirteen years later, and with millions watching him worldwide, his Irish roots were about to come out. In fact, it turned out that he was more Irish than many Irish in America. Perhaps even as Irish as many in Ireland! His aunt, Pat Bradley, explained:

We're an Irish family and we have that Irish toughness. He showed some real Bradley toughness out there and I'm just so very proud of Keegan in the way that he fought back and brought it home. He has also honoured his father who is a club pro in Wyoming.

Six times a major winner in Ladies' Golf, Pat is a member of World Golf's 'Hall of Fame'. Her grandparents hail from Ballycotton in Cork and she herself is an honorary member of Old Head and Kenmare golf clubs.

Typical of Ireland, when Irish players Harrington, McDowell and McIlroy had long since fallen out of contention for the title, Irish television back home were trumping up the chances of Irishman Bradley! Expressing his own thoughts on the matter, he said:

My family is intensely Irish. I'm very proud of my heritage and I even have a shamrock logo on my golf bag. I was over there when I was eight and I really want to go back again so bad. I want to play in the Irish Open, I really do. [His wish was granted in July 2012!]

In the meantime, Rory McIlroy could only hope that he would be the next Irishman to win the USPGA in 2012. After participating in it three times, he certainly had the formlines to win it.

But after the 2011 event, he just wanted to forget about that root of a tree on three.

****

Rory had underperformed in the first three majors of 2012 and headed to Kiawah Island in early August for the 2012 USPGA with one last chance of major success for that season. Famous for holding the Ryder Cup in 1991, it is also full of dangerous alligators.

The 186 ponds which dot the course hold one of the largest populations of the reptiles in South Carolina. It is against the law to harm any of them. Spectators are notified by the many warning notices never to approach within 60 feet of them.

The creatures can cover short distances rapidly. Spectators are also warned that it is 'strictly prohibited' to feed them with fines of $200 or 30 days in prison. 'Throwing objects' at an alligator can lead to a whopping $5,000 fine and a year's imprisonment!

Armed with a bottle of water on a humid but calm day with no hint of a breeze, Rory looked confident as he approached the 10th tee, his opening hole. The conditions were ideal for him and he could certainly tear up the course or 'shoot a number'.

So it proved as he enjoyed a really good and satisying day. There were very few mistakes in an opening round of -5, 67. One error occurred at the par-three 17th (his eighth) when his ball hit a lady and ricocheted back into a bunker. He saved par from 10 feet.

Recalling afterwards that, besides hitting the woman on the hip, he had also hit a teenager on the head at the British Open, Rory quipped: 'It's becoming a habit, hitting people in majors. I'll try not to do it again!'

The lady in question left the course very happy when McIlroy gave her a ball as a souvenir, and then Rory was asked about another lady. Ireland's Katie Taylor won a Gold medal in Boxing at the London Olympics that same day. A delighted Rory said: 'I'm so happy for her. It's not easy when everyone is expecting you to win all the time.'

There were a lot of good omens for Rory on that day. In the European Amateur championships held on the Montgomerie course at Carton House back in Ireland, fellow Northern Irelander Alan Dunbar equalled the course record with a blistering -8, 64.

Rory could not have been any happier with his own form. He was just a shot behind both Carl Peterson of Sweden and Gonzalo Fernandez-Castano of Spain after the first Round. They both shot 66. But Rory seemed sharp and focussed and said about his 67:

I'm very happy. I love the set up of this course. I got my lines right but I know that today was the easiest day we'll get as the forecast is bad with wind picking up for the weekend.

Alongside Rory on 67 were the likes of John Daly and defending champion Keegan Bradley. Rory's good buddy Graeme McDowell was in a group on 68 and Tiger Woods shot 69. Clutching another bottle of water at the subsequent Press Conference, he said:

You have to have the right attitude going out there. Every time you hit it in the middle of the green here, you're going to have a chance, especially the way the greens are rolling. For me, it's just about giving myself as many chances as possible.

So many times in golf, as in life, a bad day often follows a good one. He came right back down to earth with a nasty bump in the second round. A score of +3, 75 slipped him back to a share of fifth place on two under and two shots behind co-leaders Petersson, Woods and V J Singh.

Petersson had an over-par round as well, which bore testimony to tricky conditions after heavy bursts of rain overnight were followed by a windy, blustery day. This weather pattern would disrupt play in the penultimate round.

In fact, in the third round on Saturday, Rory was exactly halfway through his round – and a good round – when play was suspended until the following day. The leaderboard, and the world's media, would show Rory in a share of the lead at six under with Singh.

When the players returned early on Sunday morning to finish their third round, Rory and the big Fijian Singh were a shot ahead of Australian Adam Scott. By the end, at seven under, he stretched his lead to three shots over Petersson and Trevor Immelman after hitting -5, 67.

The final round was full of twists and turns and acts and episodes that no scriptwriter could even dream of. And have you ever noticed how in sport, lightning really does have this habit of striking twice, and even thrice?

Sports competitors like to term it 'luck evening itself out'. Carl Petersson was a case in point. You may recall that in the USPGA the previous year, a small boy picked up Rory's ball and left it back behind a tree.

Well incredibly and increduously, almost exactly a year later, a small child picked up Carl Petersson's ball in this final round, but not before the most amazing bad luck befell the big Swede at the very first hole.

Starting the day three shots behind Rory in second place, he incurred a two-shot penalty after he was adjudged to have touched a leaf with his club on the backswing when playing from a hazard. Touched a leaf!

Replays and replays over and over again (and slowing it right down) failed to show where the actual infringement occurred – if there was one. As Rory said himself a few years later when he was penalised: 'there are some really stupid, silly rules in golf.'

Poor Petersson ended up with a double-bogey six and viewers may have thought it was the end of him and his bad luck. But valiantly, he made a couple more birdies before he was dealt another savage cruel card.

On the sixth hole, a kid picked up the Swede's ball and when

Petersson asked for a ruling, he had to replace the ball. When he did, it ended up in a worse situation than where it had originally been.

However, whether it was his anger or frustration (or both), or loosening his elbow to have a right go, he hit back with another courageous birdie barrage. It brought him back up in the rear view mirror of the leaders but then McIlroy zoomed away again.

Rory scorched the front nine which was exactly the plan, as he told the packed press gathering afterwards. And Carl Petersson was not the only one making multiple birdies. So, take the back seat with Rory driving and hear it from his view, as he told the media:

I knew what Ian Poulter was doing (five birdies in a row to begin his round). I had a peek at a few leaderboards out there and saw he was seven under through eight or six under through seven so I knew he was off to a great start.

I set myself a target at the start of the day and said that I wanted to get to 12 under par. I got to -10 at the turn and knew I had a few opportunities on the back nine. If I played solid through 13 holes, then once I got through 13 I knew there were a couple of chances coming up and I was able to take them.

I saw with a few holes to go that I was six ahead – I think I was six ahead with six to play – and I also knew that I had two good chances coming up on 15 and 16 for birdies. You just have to stick to your game plan and not change it. And even if you do get so far ahead, you must stick to the original plan. That is what I tried to do.

He won by eight shots! A fantastic final round six under, 66, left him alone at the top of the leaderboard on 13 under. His second major, and he had also won the US Open by eight shots.

More records fell and one in particular was rolled out for a while – it being that Rory was younger than Tiger Woods when Woods captured his second major.

Actually he was only just a month behind Jack Nicklaus and three months behind Seve Ballesteros but the fact will always remain that all four – Rory, Tiger, Seve and Jack – were 23 years of age when they won their second major title.

Endless congratulations messages spewed out with Irish Taoiseach

Enda Kenny saying: 'This is further confirmation of his enormous golfing talent and a clear signal that he has the potential to become one of the greats of the game.'

Northern Ireland First Minister Peter Robinson and his Deputy First Minister Martin McGuinness weighed in with their tributes, Mr Robinson saying: 'Rory McIlroy has become the first golfer from Northern Ireland to win a second major. His golfing talent knows no bounds and who knows what he'll achieve in his career.'

Graeme McDowell led the plaudits from the Irish professionals adding: 'He's going to be a superstar of the game, which he is already, but a real superstar. He's going to be the player that kids look up to. I mean he's got great attitude, great charisma and great character. That's pretty much it in a nutshell. He's great for the game – an absolute breath of fresh air for the game.'

Padraig Harrington compared him to Tiger Woods, saying: 'Rory's proving that when he plays well, he plays like Tiger. Tiger turned up for a few years and if he brought his A-game, the rest of us struggled. Rory is now showing that with his A-game, everybody else is going to struggle to compete with him.'

Who better to have the final words on a fantastic major win (during which he beat Jack Nicklaus record margin of victory for the USPGA) than Rory himself. At the post-event press conference, he was asked what it meant after his efforts since his US Open win.

Wide-eyed like a child looking up at Santa Claus, and glaring up lovingly at the huge silver Wanamaker Trophy less than a foot away from his shoulder, he explained what had unfolded since the US Open win:

I think I made it very clear that I wasn't too happy with how I've performed in the majors since the US Open. I didn't really contend. Last Wednesday [eve of USPGA], I just talked about giving myself a chance and to be honest, that's all I wanted to do. I feel these days that when I give myself a chance to win one of these big tournaments, I can draw on the memories of Augusta, of Congressional and here today, and know what I did out there and so know what to do again. There's quite a bit of relief to get the

second one out of the way.

Then it was all over. Confined to another page of history and statistics. As for Rory's next port of call? He flew to celebrate the win with his girlfriend Caroline Wozniacki who was playing in a tennis tournament in Cincinnati.

Chapter 5

POSSESSED

In the seemingly never ending see-saw world rankings battle with Luke Donald, Rory regained the number one spot again after his USPGA triumph. On 10.35 points to Donald's 9.59, Rory actually let his true feelings known about that scenario when he revealed:

To win my second major and get to number one all in the same day is very special. I have had a little taste of it switching back and forth with Luke a couple of times. I went back down to number three and back to number one now. It's nice. It's something that completely wasn't on my mind. I just wanted to go out and try and win but it's a great bonus.

On the subject of how he would rate his game, Rory was asked what grade he would give himself for the season. Without any hesitation he responded emphatically:

'A1'. I heard Tiger Woods once say that to have a good season, you need a major championship. Now I've had two great seasons in a row, no matter what happens from here on in. Hopefully I can play some great golf from now until the end of the year. And get myself ready for another great season next year too.

When Rory returned to the US Tour on 23 August, exactly two weeks after his stunning USPGA win, very few who know the game expected him to win The Barclays. It is extremely rare for a major winner to turn out and win in their next event.

It is a fact that being a major winner means that wherever you go, and whenever you pop your head out, people rush to smile, offer handshakes and blurt out their well wishes of congratulations.

This is particularly in evidence at the next golf tournament. So many of the players want to offer their hand and the back patting never stops. It has the effect of making the major winner feel that they are still in celebration mode. Still up there on 'cloud nine'.

Even at press conferences before, during and after The Barclays, the media just want to know about the major win – and all the questions about being younger than Tiger and the same age as Nicklaus and Ballesteros. Rory duly finished tied for 24th place on one under.

One week later on 30 August, he teed off in another of the Fedex Cup events: the Deutsche Bank championship in Boston. He got off to a great start to boot with a -6, 65. This put him just a shot behind co-leaders Tiger Woods, Jeff Overton and Ryan Moore.

It was significant to see the mighty name of Tiger Woods up in lights again and leading a big event. In the previous weeks he had actually leapt over Lee Westwood to be number three in the world and that, together with his 64, showed that he was still a major force.

The next day McIlroy started his second round at the 10th and he began in the same form as he had finished the day before. He was on fire. At the 12th he birdied from 18 feet, his second shot finished a foot from the pin for birdie at the 14th and he sank another five-foot birdie at 15.

Rory then eagled the 18th and made yet another birdie at the first to be six under for his round after just ten holes and -12 for the tournament. The run came to an end with two bogeys, before two more back-to-back birdies meant he shot another -6, 65.

It was the best opening two rounds that Rory had produced for some time and it gave him a one shot lead over Tiger Woods going into the weekend. At the halfway point this was his reaction:

I'm very pleased with how I played today, how I played yesterday as well, and in a great position going into the weekend. I got off to a nice start and sort of just kept the momentum going. So yeah, everything seemed to work pretty well out there. I felt like I drove the ball a bit better today and hit more fairways, which gave me some more opportunities to make birdies, and I was putting well enough to take a few of those.

Rory could not keep it going however. He slipped back a little after a 67 moved him to -16 and three shots behind the big mover on moving day – Louis Oosthuizen. The slender framed South African upstaged Rory, Tiger and the entire field with a fabulous -8, 63.

So there was to be no all-star final pairing of Woods and McIlroy for the romantics.

Instead, Rory would have that honour with Oosthuizen but he had three shots to make up. He did get off to a flier, as the quiet and affable South African had a day to forget.

Oosthuizen made far too many errors and resulting bogeys. Although he clawed his way back and made some birdies on the way home to get within a shot of Rory, the damage was done.

He made another bogey on the 17th as did Rory but after he failed to birdie the final hole, meaning Rory just had to make par, it was all over. Rory had won his third event of the year in America and he was thrilled:

I'm delighted to have won my fifth PGA title, and third this year. Going out today I knew that I had to put a little bit of pressure on Louis and I think I did that. I was able to do that playing the first holes three under, and we both made a couple of mistakes on the fifth hole, but he made a six to my five, so I was able to take advantage of that a little bit.

The win brought Rory's earnings on the US Tour alone to well over $6 million dollars for the season, with more events to play. On the European Tour he amassed almost €4 million so he was also in line to do what Luke Donald had done and win both Money Lists.

He had stretched his lead significantly at the top of the world rankings but another golfer was making big noises on and off the course. A certain Tiger Woods finished just two shots behind Rory in third place. Later, he warned the world he was getting better and better.

Three days later Rory arrived in Carmel, Indiana, (not to be confused with Carmel on the Monterrey peninsula in California, home of Hollywood legend Clint Eastwood) for the BMW Championship.

Rain in the preceding days had made the 'Crooked Stick' course soft, which was just the way Rory preferred it. After so much play in hot, humid conditions and on hard and sun baked courses, this meant Rory could 'use' the ball by putting backspin on it.

His rich vein of form continued as he pummeled the fairways and greens with a -8, 64. Teeing off at the 10th, he picked up a few early birdies and had his only bogey of the day on the 13th. However, his round really kicked into gear when he eagled the par-five 15th.

Birdies on his last two holes at the 8th and 9th capped off a very good day with a delighted Rory telling the media after his round:

It was great. With the soft conditions you could really shoot a number out there and I did. I took advantage of also hitting the ball really well, hitting it in the fairway which I need to do and also hitting it long and giving myself a lot of opportunities. I missed a few but was able to make the most of them. Great start to the tournament.

Joining him at the top after the first round were Canadian Graham DeLaet and Americans Webb Simpson and Bo Van Pelt. Ominously placed just a shot behind – and as good as his word of improving – was Tiger Woods, along with Luke Donald.

Woods, who partnered Rory for the day, actually chipped in from 30 feet for a birdie on the last hole. When he came in to face the media, he gave a huge ringing endorsement of young Rory having seen him up close in the heat of battle. These were Tiger's words:

He's a nice kid, he really is. It's fun to play with him and he's just an amazing talent. You watch him swing the club and watch him putt and play – he doesn't have a lot of weaknesses. This is the next generation of guys coming out. You can see that, in the next decade or so, as he really matures and understands some of the nuances of the game, he's only going to get better. And that's fun to see. The game of golf is in great hands with him and he's here to stay.

With such glowing words from one of the best players to have graced the game, you would have expected an inspired Rory to leave the field in his slipstream. But after his 64, he regressed over the next two days with rounds of 68, 69 to lie on 15 under.

Phil Mickelson matched Rory's best of the week 64 in the third round, and so he was the overnight leader with Vijay Singh going into the final day. Rory would go out in the second-to-last group with his old pal Lee Westwood.

Fijian Singh, who has struggled to get back to his best over the past few years, was the first to crack and never really struck a blow. His playing partner 'Lefty' Mickelson also faltered and despite finishing with his usual late flurry, he did not trouble the principals.

It proved to be another appetizing gun fight between Rory and Westy as James Corrigan of The Telegraph pointed out:

It seemed appropriate that golf's finest topped one of golf's finest leader boards. While McIlroy and Westwood went at it like two heavyweights, prizefighters of the quality of Tiger Woods, Mickelson, Dustin Johnson and Vijay Singh threw their own shots. However, as hard as they tried none of them could bring down the 23-year-old.

Westwood gave McIlroy a real grilling. After a series of stunning approach shots, he kept pace with Rory up until the 13th hole when they were neck and neck in a terrific duel. Then Rory upped another gear and pulled away.

His birdies on the 15th and 16th were true examples of a real champion under pressure. Everything that was thrown at him he took and gave it back with an extra thud. Those two birdies proved the difference with McIlroy winning by two shots from Westwood.

A late birdie from Mickelson lifted him to a share of second place with the valiant Englishman on -18. Tiger Woods was a further shot back tied for fourth on -17. Rory, in just one week, hit winning scores of -20 to win the Deutsche Bank and BMW – 40 under par!

Two wins in a week and three wins in a month. Rory McIlroy was in dreamland. Never mind winning $2.9 million in that week, he was now leading the Fedex Cup rankings and was in line for a cool

$10 million if he remained top by the end of the following week.

The press conferences were now becoming almost giddy. Rory probably entered those rooms seeing the same faces and running out of things to say. If the truth is known, so were the scribes! For the record, this was his reaction after the BMW win:

I'm on a great run at the minute. I actually had to scramble a bit out there but I drove the ball beautifully today. It's great to be able to win events like these when the quality [of the field] is so good. I came here with the mindset from Boston that I just wanted to keep going on this roll. Some suggested that I could take a week off and still be in the Top 5 of the Fedex Cup going into Atlanta but I felt I was playing really well and didn't want to stop. I sort of picked up from where I left in Boston, shooting 64 the first day here, and I'm playing with a lot of confidence right now. I'm confident in my ability and with the shots that I'm hitting and confident on the greens. I'm making the right decisions out there and everything is just going to plan at the minute. I want to try and keep it going for as long as possible.

Alas Rory was to be floored by a knockout uppercut at the season's final event, the Tour Championship. The rains had been to Rory's advantage in the previous event but the winds put a huge dent in his challenge and in his bid to win the Fedex Cup.

After four quick bogeys on the front nine, the writing was on the wall. Brandt Snedeker, who had been most consistent in the four Fedex Cup events, came through to win by three shots from Justin Rose and claim the whopping $10 million prize.

An argument could have sprung up and raged as to the merits of 'consistency' versus 'wins' to decide the outcome of the Fedex Cup. After all, Rory had won twice. But it is as it is and similar parameters can be drawn with boxing – a win by knockout or points.

Snedeker was runner-up in The Barclays when Rory only tied 24th and he was a consistent high finisher in the previous two that Rory won. A final round 74 from Rory and tied 10th was his undoing. He hid his severe disappointment afterwards when saying:

I'm a little disappointed, but at the same time, Brandt really deserves to win. He played the best golf out of anyone. He knew what he needed to do. He needed to come in here and win. He controlled his own destiny, just like I did. And he was able to come and do that. So because of that, he really deserves it.

Make no mistake about it, Rory is a winner and this hurt – big time. The key words in that statement, which showed that he felt he should have been the victor, and perhaps that the Fedex Cup should be on a 'win basis', was his 'just like I did'.

McIlroy would dearly love to have joined Tiger Woods (twice), Vijay Singh, Jim Furyk and Bill Haas as the only men to have won the Fedex Cup since its inception in 2007. But it was Brandt Snedeker, and in another respect, Brandt was a most deserving winner.

In these modern times when there is a growing worldwide call for millionaires and billionaires to give away some or most of their fortunes (as they can still live securely on the rest of it) to worthwhile causes, then the Tennessee golfer was a real winner.

This is what he said after his win and it was really one of the quotes of the year:

I'm not by any means a flashy guy. Of anybody that I know, I do not need $10 million. So there are going to be things that we can really do to help people. So that's the way I look at it. This is unbelievable, to be financially stable for the rest of my career. As long as I'm not an idiot, I should be fine. But I really think we can make a difference and help a lot of Nashville and Tennessee people out.

It was not the colossal amount of money Rory felt disappointed to lose out on. After all, he had just added a further $3 million to his bank balance after finishing second to Snedeker in the Fedex Cup rankings.

Moreover, it was the fact that he was now a winner and as such, when he is in sight of breaking a record or winning some bonus on top of the event he is participating in, then he wants to add that as well. You could term it the 'tiddlywinks factor'.

There was only one other tournament that mattered to Rory for the rest of the year, and that was coming up fast in less than three weeks. There was no playing for dollars or euros here – this was for pride and patriotism. It was the 39th Ryder Cup at Medinah, Illinois.

That is a whole new chapter so in finishing out the bread and butter tour business for 2012, Rory's form held up very well and as the season drew to a close in Europe, he finished with even more success.

At the BMW Masters in China towards the end of October, he sparkled with four superb rounds of 67, 65, 69 and 67 for 20 under yet again. But he came up just short and was runner-up to Swede Peter Hanson. Rory collected a whopping second prize of €593,000!

Two weeks later it was back to Asia for the Singapore Open. An early round of -1, 70 really did the damage as Rory fell off the pace. But he finished strongly with rounds of 69 and a superb -6, 65 to finish third and collect another handsome cheque for just short of €300,000.

All the traveling and gargantuan efforts of the previous weeks and months eventually took their toll – or so one would have thought when he missed the cut in the Hong Kong Open the following week.

But at the World Tour Championship in Dubai exactly seven days later, and in his last event of the year, McIlroy triumphed yet again for his fifth win of a truly sensational season.

The rounds and the cumulative total just put the icing on the cake of what he had achieved throughout the year. 66, 67, 66 and 66 for 23 under was near perfection. He won by two shots from Justin Rose, with Donald and Schwartzel three shots adrift of Rose.

Some of those very players paid huge tributes to McIlroy after their rounds. South African Schwartzel stated: 'Rory is playing like Tiger in his young days and it's amazing to see.'

Fellow countryman Louis Oosthuizen echoed similar sentiments: 'Rory is probably playing the golf that Tiger was playing when he was on form.'

And Luke Donald really summed up what everyone felt when he added: 'He showed a lot of grit and determination. It capped off an amazing year for him. Rory has been the best player all year. I think he'll be around for a long time.'

Both sides of the Atlantic echoed what Donald said.

After winning the US Tour Money List and the European Order of Merit, it was no surprise that he was also voted European Player of the Year as well as winning the PGA of America's Player of the Year and its Vardon Trophy for lowest scoring average.

That Dubai pay day of €1,041,000 brought Rory's earnings on the European Tour alone to €5 million from 12 events played. His US Tour earnings amounted to a colossal $11 million - $8 million in tour money plus the Fedex bonus of $3 million.

However, those millions were nothing compared to the imminent multi-million dollar deal that Rory was expected to sign with Nike after he had rested up for Christmas, for the win in Dubai was his last as a Titleist player.

Decades from now when Rory puts his clubs away in the garage, he will look back on 2012 as one of the greatest years of his career.

Chapter 6

SEVE'S MIRACLE OF MEDINAH
(2012 Ryder Cup Part 1)

He may have gone into the previous Ryder Cup in 2010 on the back of rash, immature and controversial remarks that he uttered in the past, but Rory McIlroy was now about to enter the bear pit of America's backyard with their full and unambiguous respect.

Professional golfers the length and breadth of the globe were doubtless in awe of this unbelievable talent. Furthermore, there is always a feeling in sport that if you're going to talk, or make controversial remarks, then back up your talk in the heat of competition.

Rory had done that. More than that, he had realised the inappropriateness and immaturity of his remarks about Tiger and the Cup being an exhibition. So rather than talk about them again – or dwell on it – he just forgot the talk, and he walked the walk.

The Holywood man was about to strutt into Medinah, outside Chicago, as a Ryder Cup treasure. He was winner of five events; winner of both money lists; winner of both Tours' 'player of the year' and as world number one he was officially the best player on view.

This did not mean that the Americans had no ammunition of their own. Rory, after all, is only one man in a twelve man team. The USA had the all important home advantage which had proved so crucial to Europe on the last occasion in Wales 2010.

The likeable and very popular Jose Maria Olazabal was the new European Captain. Although it was officially announced on 18 January 2011, there was really no need to do so.

Thomas Bjorn echoed the situtaion when saying 'it was the easiest decision ever'. In fact, it was so straightforward that the Ryder Cup

Committee did not have to hold any meetings, nor did they feel any need to debate the matter.

From the outset, there was only one thing the Committee wanted to know from Olazabal – was his health holding up (he suffers from rheumatoid arthritis)? When he gave them a clean bill on that issue, the selection proccess was a formality.

It was an easy decision for one vital reason – he was the Vice Captain under Colin Montgomerie in the victorious 2010 team and he was seen to play a huge part in that win. Although captaincy was an altogether more demanding role, he was the only choice.

J M Olazabal therefore became only the third Continental European, and the second from Spain, to become a European Ryder Cup Captain, following in the paths of Severiano Ballesteros and Bernhard Langer. On his appointment he said:

Golf has been my life and representing Europe in the Ryder Cup has given me so much enjoyment, so to be named the European Ryder Cup captain is something very special and I am looking forward to the next 20 months before we reach Medinah.

A masterstroke was also played at his press conference when he cleared any potential trouble spots up ahead in the future, or indeed at the Ryder Cup itself. He showed that he was a pacifist and that sleeves would be rolled up for golf only, adding:

I've spent a lot of my career in America and the fans there have always been fair to me. We want to keep the Cup and that will be our priority but I know the American team will share with us the desire for this match to continue the fabulous tradition of the Ryder Cup with fair play and good sportsmanship as the vital ingredients.

With those very words he not only threw a protecting arm around his players, like Rory, and the American players, but he also laid to rest the ghosts of past 'unsavoury' Ryder Cups involving the likes of himself, Sevy, Pavin, Lehman, Azinger, and indeed McIlroy.

'Ollie', as he is affectionately known to all in golf, was not only a two-time major winner of the US Masters, to add to his Ryder Cup successes, he was also a real fighter with balls of fire.

Down through the years he had proved this as he forged a virtually indefatigible winning partnership with Severiano Ballesteros in many Ryder Cups. They had only lost two of 15 ties, so a long line of American team members wanted to avoid Seve and Ollie at all costs.

Apart from that steely will to win, on and off the course, Olazabal was determined right from the outset to bring into play the 'spirit of Seve'. When Seve passed away four months later on 7 May the world of golf mourned and many, like Sam Torrance, wept openly.

As was only to be expected, Olazabal was affected most by the death of his close friend. They were like brothers. Even now, if Seve is brought up in conversation, his mood will dampen.

At his funeral, Jose Maria Olazabal was determined that the memory of Severiano Ballesteros would not be forgotten. Silently, there and then, he vowed to do everything to bring Seve's memory and spirit into play on behalf of the European team at Medinah.

It was to be a staggering and stunning ploy. But the real beauty of it was that it was not a tactic: it was a real tool to use. It was genuine. Where golfers or other athletes can use physical skill and intelligence to win, Ollie would use Seve's spirit. Plain and simple.

Short of suggesting that he was using seances and ouija boards for much needed guidance and inspiration from Seve, he would in actual fact use the hard earned experience of real grit, determination, fire and fight that he and Seve had shown.

At every opportunity he would use this first hand experience and instill it into each and every one of his players. It was not brainwashing or euphoria. Rather, it was a beautiful manual handed down from him and Seve of 'how to win on the hot battlefield'.

In the meantime, and with fully a year and more to the big day, he had to monitor the progress of every European player at home and in the US. Then all the names had to be whittled down resulting in the announcement of his team and wildcards, totalling 12.

****

Rory McIlroy 468.81; Luke Donald 363.4; Justin Rose 322.3; Lee Westwood 280.2; Graeme McDowell 262.62; Paul Lawrie 211.49;

Sergio Garcia 200.85; Francesco Molinari 191.25; Peter Hanson 189.32 and Martin Kaymer 172.2.

They were the automatic Top 10 European players with Ryder Cup points who made it to Medinah. At his eagerly awaited press conference on 27th August, 2012 to announce his full team, it only remained for him to name his wildcards. This is what he revealed:

Every one of you guessed Ian [Poulter] was going to be there for obvious reasons. He has a great Ryder Cup record, he was playing well – he had some issues earlier in the season, he got ill and he couldn't play as much – but he is cured and his attitude and spirit in the Ryder Cup team has always been great. He likes to be in that situation, it gets the best out of him playing in the Ryder Cup.

To finish, Nicolas Colsaerts became the first Belgian to be named in a Ryder Cup team. He was also the only rookie in the side which raised quite a few eyebrows. Explaining his decision to pick him, Olazabal said:

His matchplay record is very good. He also had a very solid season. On top of that he made the extra effort to try to make the team. He showed me he wanted to be part of the team.

Regarding some top players who failed to make it – including Padraig Harrington who was touted by some to be a 'Captains pick' – Olazabal elaborated on the omission of the Dubliner saying:

I talked to him last night and I was very straight and to the point. I know he's tried hard but he was 19th, just a little too far down the list. I know he's a great player. I'd love to have had him in the team as I'd also love to have had Casey, Karlsson, Stenson – great players – but you need to be playing good. It's as simple as that. I think he took it well.

Nicolas Colsaerts was thrilled and gave this memorable reaction:

This is something I've wanted since I was a kid – to be part of a big

*team with a captain with such a great history. It's something I'm
very proud of. I'm living proof that if you want something badly
it's only a matter of time if you put the work in. It's a fairy story.*

Little did Ian Poulter know what lay in store for him at Medinah.
The 'obvious reasons' which Olazabal made reference to in his
announcement lay in the fact that the Englishman had won seven of
his eight previous Ryder Cup games. Poulter said: 'I'm absolutely
thrilled to have got the call last night from Jose. It was a great
moment.'

American Captain Davis Love had a very strong looking American
team. With the likes of Tiger Woods, Phil Mickelson, Steve Stricker,
Jim Furyk, Bubba Watson, Zach Johnson and Keegan Bradley, they
seemed formidable.

Add to those names men like gritty Brandt Snedeker and Jason
Dufner and they did not seem to have any weaknesses in the personnel
department. It was easy to see why the bookmakers installed USA as
the four to six favourites, with Europe at six to four.

Almost exactly a month later, battle commenced. Rory would
stride into Medinah, making his second Ryder Cup appearance in
the 38th version of golf's greatest team event. It was also his Ryder
Cup debut in America.

On the eve of the first day's play, Rory was asked about the
American tactics. More to the point, he was asked his views on their
tactics concerning who they would select to play against him in the
foursomes. This was his reply:

*Whoever wants to take me on they can take me on. I just
want to get out and get a point for the team. Whether that
means going out first, fourth or in the middle, it really doesn't
make a difference to me and it doesn't make any difference
who I play. I'm going to go out there and do my best and
win that point. I don't think I have a bullseye on my back.
This week I'm not the world number one – I'm one person in a 12
man team and that's it.*

As it transpired, Rory was out first. Surprisingly, there was no Tiger

Woods or Phil Mickeslon pitted against him and his usual playing partner, Graeme McDowell. Davis Love opted instead to put Jim Furyk and Brandt Snedeker out first.

Just what is it about this competition that, no matter what the authorities do to try to dampen down or prevent any potential hostilities or flash points, controversy is never too far away? We did not have long to wait for the first niggly and awkward moment.

On the second hole, McDowell had sought relief from a sprinkler head but Jim Furyk disagreed with him! A rules official had to be called for and he ultimately sided with the Americans, denying McDowell any relief.

The Americans went on to win the hole. Inwardly, the two Macs must have been livid and left somewhat embarrassed by being confronted. However, this is what Jim Furyk had to say about the incident afterwards:

I saw that he was going to get relief. I went over and when I looked to see where the ball was, it was a good – and I'm being conservative – four to five inches ahead of the sprinkler head. So they would get a big advantage by being able to drop the ball. He had a sticky lie and a very delicate chip and to be able to putt that ball would have been a huge advantage and I really didn't feel in any situation, whether it be matchplay or medal play that it could be deemed a drop. As I told Graeme and Rory, 'I don't blame you for trying, for asking – 'trying' is a bad word – for 'asking'. Graeme then said to me 'I thought it was 50/50 but you're entitled to your opinion'. I'm not trying to incite any tension or bother anyone but it's my job for my team mates and for my team to protect ourselves and the rules.

Professional golfers are generally honest and there is no reason to suggest here that anybody was trying to cheat or gain an unfair advantage. Earlier in the book we saw how Luke Donald questioned Rory over his ball and Rory was penalised as a result.

The 'Macs' felt it was 50/50 and that was fair. The Americans felt the ball was far enough away from the sprinkler that it did not constitute a free drop – also fair. So I contacted well known European Tour referee John Paramor about the case.

Now, there is no actual direct reference to 'sprinkler heads' (nor has there ever been) in the updated Rules of Golf. So, this is what John Paramor told me and it seems evident that he would have done the exact same thing as the referee who ruled that day:

Sprinkler heads are obstructions by definition - anything artificial - and clearly it is immovable. Therefore Rule 24-2 applies and if a sprinkler head interferes with a player's stance or area of intended swing, the player is entitled to relief without penalty. If the player wishes to take relief, he must find the nearest point where there is no longer any interference from the obstruction and drop his ball within one club-length of this point, not nearer the hole or on a putting green. In the Ryder Cup match you cite, the player felt there was interference to his intended swing but Jim Furyk and the referee disagreed.

Graeme and Rory's reaction stunned the Yanks who must have regretted calling for the referee. The Northern Ireland aces went on a spree winning five out of eight holes to the 11th. They found themselves 3-up with the Americans shell shocked and running out of holes.

The glorious unpredictability of the Cup and all its pressures took hold again. The Europeans then faltered in the face of an American blitzkrieg. After winning three out of four holes both teams were back where they began at the very first hole – all square.

As the four golfers and their caddies stood on the 18th tee, ready to give their all one last time, you could hear a pin drop. The pressure, as only this event can throw up, must have been enormous.

Something had to give. Would it be the Irish pair who had squandered a handsome 3-up lead, or would the Yanks continue their momentum and win the day? Brandt Snedeker cracked.

He hit a very poor drive off the tee and as hard as Jim Furyk tried to retrieve the situation, he could not. They bogeyed the hole and a par from McDowell was enough for the Europeans to win the very first tie of 2012, 1-up.

Rory had another precious point on his Ryder resume but there was no time to gloat or go to the media and tell how it was. Tieing in with typical tradition, he and G-Mac headed back out on the course to show support to their team mates.

By the end of the morning foursome session, both teams were tied at two points each. Phil Mickelson and Keegan Bradley inflicted a first ever defeat on Luke Donald in foursomes. He and Sergio Garcia were well and truly put in their place and lost 4 and 3.

The USA then took the lead when Jason Dufner and Zach Johnson defeated Lee Westwood and Francesco Molinari 3 and 2. However, wildcard Ian Poulter came to Europe's rescue as he and Justin Rose enjoyed a thrilling 2 and 1 win over Tiger Woods and Steve Stricker.

McIlroy and McDowell went out again for the afternoon fourballs where they faced a daunting task taking on Phil Mickelson and Keegan Bradley who had been awesome against Garcia and Donald.

After just a few holes things were looking bad, as all around the course the local crowds were hollering themselves into a right frenzy. Mickelson and Bradley began where they left off and tore into the Irishmen.

They were 3-up through three holes and then 4-up through the eighth hole. Although that deficit was cut to 2-down, Mickelson sealed victory on the 17th with another one of his moments of magic and genius.

Standing over his tee shot at the 193-yard par three and seeing water all around the front of the green, and with Rory and G-Mac and Bradley standing looking at him, he unleashed his shot high over Lake Kadijah.

When his ball landed, the greatest explosion of noise reverberated all over the course like a cannon booming off. You know that noise you hear – 'plump' or 'thud' – when you are in the vicinity of a ball land on a green. Well, this was neither. It was a 'boom'!

The match was over. Lefty's ball finished stone dead three feet from the pin. All four players shook hands after neither European ever looked like obtaining an unlikely hole-in-one to half the match. The American pair won 2 and 1.

It had been a most memorable day for Keegan Bradley and Phil Mickelson and their day was made complete when two more USA pairings secured wins. In the first match out, Bubba Watson and Webb Simpson slaughtered poor Peter Hanson and Paul Lawrie 5 and 4.

Then two big surprises unfolded. Firstly, Dustin Johnson and Matt Kuchar easily beat Justin Rose and Martin Kaymer 3 and 2, before the European Captain's second wildcard choice helped to save the day for Europe.

Nicolas Colsaerts enjoyed a dream debut as he and Lee Westwood secured an unlikely looking win over mighty Tiger Woods and Steve Stricker. The US looked set to win that tie, before losing it to Europe on the very last hole.

That proved to be one of the turning points in what would eventually turn out to be a gripping Ryder Cup. Europe trailed by two points overnight after the first day's play, but as Rory McIlroy stated afterwards:

It's not actually that bad and for a while this afternoon it looked like it was going to be a very bad day. We're only two points behind with eight to play for on Saturday so we're still in a decent position. We're pretty strong on foursomes so if we get a good start in the morning and even things up that would be great.

Davis Love created a sensation when he announced his Saturday morning foursomes next day. He dropped Tiger Woods. Now it can be dressed up and camouflaged in any manner the American Captain sees fit but the fact is Woods (and Stricker) were dropped.

Tiger was deemed not to be the player to help increase the United States lead as he was not in good enough form. He and Stricker lost their two matches the previous day. Tiger would instead be brought into the afternoon fourballs.

Europe got off to the perfect required start on Saturday when Ian Poulter and Justin Rose again showed great tenacious fighting spirit to pip Bubba Watson and Webb Simpson on the last hole.

That was as good as it got for Europe that morning. The lethal cocktail of Keegan Bradley and Phil Mickelson absolutely destroyed Lee Westwood and Luke Donald 7 and 6. That was a real eye opener as the English pair had always been seen as so strong.

America had restored their two point advantage and they increased it to three points when Zach Johnson and Jason Duffner beat Sergio Garcia and Nicolas Colsaerts 2 and 1. The last match of the morning was crucial for Europe with Rory and Graeme facing Furyk and Snedeker again!

The Americans got off to the perfect start when winning the first hole and they maintained that advantage. Furyk and Snedeker were rock steady from tee to green as McDowell struggled.

The Europeans cut a 2-down deficit to just one with an impressive birdie on the 16th but Rory's birdie attempt on the par-three 17th slid just by the edge. It was another tight encounter that went the distance with the Americans playing 1-up at the last.

On the 18th veteran Furyk, who has come under intense scrutiny for his lacklustre record in the Cup, zipped a sand wedge from a fairway bunker to put his partner in prime putting position.

Snedeker, who made the team on account of his tremendous putting, rolled the putt to within gimme range to close out a 1-up win. It had been a bad morning for Europe, similar to the previous afternoon, as the States stretched their lead to eight to four.

In the afternoon fourballs it looked like curtains for Europe when Bubba Watson and Webb Simpson hammered Rose and Molinari 5 and 4, which preceded Dustin Johnson and Matt Kuchar's last gasp 1-up win over a desperately unlucky Colsaerts and Lawrie.

'10-4, over and out' as the radio call signals the end. Next up were the bruised and battered Woods and Stricker versus Donald and Garcia. This match gave Olazabal and Europe real hope as all four golfers had been struggling thus far, particularly Woods and Stricker.

It was a 50/50 match that Europe had to win. If they lost, United States may as well have been crowned champions. It was that simple. Europe initially answered Ollie's call. They battered the Americans for the first half.

Thanks in large part to consecutive birdies from Donald on the eighth and ninth, Europe held a commanding 4-up lead. Then at the 10th, Tiger responded with his first birdie of the day. Stricker hit another birdie at the 12th and when Woods birdied 13 Europe were just 1-up.

Donald took the wind out of their sails with a birdie on the 15th after Tiger had a disappointing miss. But Woods came back on the 16th with his fourth birdie on the back nine to bring the Americans even closer at just 1-down.

The pressure was very much on Europe. In a match they had to win, they had squandered a 4-up lead and all the momentum was with Woods and Stricker. Then, after Garcia missed his birdie on the final hole, Stricker stepped forward with a birdie putt to halve the match.

He missed! The ball shaved the hole and to Europe's immense relief, they won 1-up. It was 10-5 to the Yanks and all eyes would now switch to McIlroy and new partner Poulter.

Chapter 7

RORY AVOIDS RYDER DISQUALIFICATION!
(2012 Ryder Cup Part 2)

Rory McIlroy would go on to create one of the most bizarre and unprecedented final day incidents on the climactic Sunday of the 2012 Ryder Cup, but before that, he was involved in one of the all-time greatest Ryder Cup matches on the Saturday evening. It was an epic.

Sergio Garcia and Luke Donald were pitted against Woods and Stricker in a must-win match to prevent Europe falling 11-4 down with one match remaining. There was huge relief as they held on to win on the 18th after Stricker's birdie putt just missed.

That one game left involved McIlroy, minus his long term partner McDowell and now paired with Ian Poulter. Olazabal left out G-Mac who was suffering from fatigue after a below average display in his losing morning foursomes.

Playing Jason Dufner and Zach Johnson, the European pair did not seem to be gelling very well as Dufner and Johnson led for much of the rubber. Rory and Ian were 2-down through 12 holes.

Poulter then rolled in a beautiful long birdie on the 14th and after winning the previous hole as well, they were all square. On the 15th, the Englishman saved the day again when playing a majestic bunker shot up and down for par.

Yet another birdie on 16, after a fantastic iron shot to 15 feet, put Europe 1-up for the first time after Zach Johnson's effort for a half rolled past. With just two holes left to play, the United States battled back and birdied the 17th.

However, Europe had a birdie chance on that same hole. After a great iron shot to 10 feet, Poulter rammed home the putt and he roared and clenched his fist. It was only a half but his emotions told everyone that it was a step nearer to victory. There was one hole left.

'The Poulter Show' was even more remarkable considering the torrent of abuse and taunts that he, much more so than Rory, was receiving from disrespectful American 'fans' hiding in the cover of large crowds.

Dufner and Johnson would not give up. Disgruntled at losing their two hole lead and riled by Poulter's deranged eyes and clenched fists, they stood firm with terrific resolve. So much so that when Dufner rolled in a marvellous birdie on that final hole, America went wild.

They looked very likely to secure a half and maintain the five point lead they had coming into the match. It was well into evening now and the dew was setting on the grass which made Ian Poulter's next putt even more difficult.

Again, it was for a half but a half to give Europe a 1-up win. It was a putt of fully 10 of the longest feet Poulter, McIlroy and Europe had ever seen. On the plus side, he was in the zone. His adrenalin was sky high and he was playing brilliantly.

Make the putt, and Europe would be 10–6 behind overnight going into the last day Singles. Miss it, and America would get a crucial half-point and that five point lead. TV cameras, press cameras and microphones awaited the moment as he stood over the ball.

All the players and captains from both teams were gathered on the green, standing next to friends, wives and girlfriends. 'Sweet hair!' someone yelled as he lined it up. Then just as his putter hit the ball, one last insult echoed out from somewhere, 'Nice shoes!"

As the ball travelled you could hear hundreds of motorised zooms from cameras like a swarm of bees. It fell in the hole. There were shrieks, gasps and groans from the hugely partisan crowd and yelps and cheers from the European contingent.

Poulter turned around and as McIlroy walked swiftly over to offer an outstretched wrist, and then to hug him, the look from Poulter said it all. The mad stare from his eyes went straight through Rory as if saying to him 'who are you – where did you come from?'

It was as if he was so totally focussed on sinking the putt that he had no connection whatsoever to his team mate. He was in a different world. His body was drugged with such a toxic mix of adrenalin, euphoria, determination and relief that he was numb.

By God what a performance from Poulter that day! From Rory as well – and from Garcia and Donald – but everything depended on Poulter sinking that putt. 10-6 down, they still had a chance and the efforts of Poulter would do nothing but inspire Europe.

A third match for Poulter and a 100% record of three wins. The way he was performing Olazabal would surely have to put him out as the lead man in the Singles the following day – or would he?

He was so reminiscent of Severiano Ballesteros. A paler version perhaps, but he had similar traits like his gritting of teeth and his dogged single-minded determination to win and get the job done. It was as if Seve had infiltrated his very being.

Later that evening after the European team had freshened up and eaten, Ollie called all the players into a room for the traditional final team talk. It was the most emotional Ryder Cup team meeting ever held and what came out of there were buckets of tears.

Olazabal called on his players to follow the spirit of Seve. What Poulter had shown, in that regard, the entire team was asked to follow suit. If each of them gave 100%, it was still possible they could win.

An Indian war dance; a call to arms; a call to battle – on Sunday, there would be no need for war paint on faces. Every last one of the 12 disciples would be armed with frightening eyes that would scare and stare the bejaysus out of the Yankees and Confederates.

Their concentrated minds and eyes – using Poulter as the flagship – would beat the Americans into submission. Staring, focussing, concentrating, achieving the victory and then it was meeting over, good night.

One wonders how Rory slept. As the final day singles teed off, Ollie buzzed around the place. His eyes were darting around looking and observing. Every now and again he would ask a caddy, a golfer or anyone, in his Spanish twang, 'have you seen Rory?

Maybe McIlroy was on the range; maybe the putting green or perhaps he was in any number of quiet corners giving a radio or television interview. 'Ah don't worry Ollie, he's around somewhere – how is Luke Donald performing?'

Luke was first man out at 11.03 am against Bubba Watson and would be followed 11 minutes later by Paul Lawrie and then 11 minutes after that by Rory. But Olazabal knew something was wrong. With all his enquiries completed, Rory was not on the golf course.

In fact, McIlroy was still in his hotel room! He had misjudged his tee time by fully one hour. Whatever he was doing in there, he was oblivious to all the missed calls on both his mobile and the room phone at his bedside.

Perhaps he was listening to music on his head phones or taking a shower. When he was finally reached, he got the most almighty shock of his life. The voice on the other end was his manager Conor Ridge who told him he had less than half an hour 'til play.

If he was late, he would forfeit a point to the United States and almost certainly hand the Ryder Cup to them. Forfeiting his match would be a catastrophic disaster not even worth thinking about. A career blighted by infamy.

Rory explained later how he had so clumsily miscalculated his tee time. He told everyone consistently that he had seen his tee time as 12.25. In point of fact, his tee time was 11.25 am. But he was right – he did see 12.25 and this is why:

Most of the major news channels in the US are run by NBC or Fox who have their headquarters in New York City. Any times they give – or have down in information like sub titles and teletext – are in Eastern Time.

ET incorporates 17 US States including the East Coast of Canada. They are one hour ahead of where Rory was in Chicago. He was in Central Time zone. So wherever Rory saw his 12.25 tee time, he read it or heard it from an ET source.

He arrived at 11.14 just as Lawrie and Snedeker were teeing off. As he scrambled out of the Police car, a crowd of American fans saw him and started chanting 'Central Time Zone'! He smiled with embarrassment and held his hand up to acknowledge them.

Had his patrol car become stuck in traffic, and Rory arrived on the tee at 11.26 which was one minute after his tee off time, he would still have been allowed to play. But 11.30 or thereafter would have been curtains. Top referee John Paramor explained it to me:

With regard to Rory arriving late on the tee, we would have used Rule 6-3a in the Rule book - loss of first hole up to five minutes and thereafter DQ. We used to use a graduated scale of penalty but that was some time ago.

In other words, Rory not being on time at 11.25 still meant he would have been allocated an additional five minutes for the loss of the first hole – i.e. Bradley 1-up (strokeplay = two-shot penalty). If there was no sign of Rory after five minutes, he would have been disqualified.

Later he told the press corps how he had got there so quickly. He explained:

I was just casually strolling out of my hotel room when I got a phone call saying 'you have 25 minutes to get here'. I have never been so worried driving to the course. Luckily there was a state trooper outside who gave me the escort. If not I would not have made it on time. I was putting on my golf shoes in the car beside him.

The warning signs were also there for Rory in a previous escape. Earlier in the season when he won his second major the USPGA by eight shots, there was a weather delay. So he decided to go to his Florida home to sleep and come back later.

In that USPGA at Kiawah Island, he had played nine holes of his third round and so had to play 27 on the last day. So he dashed from Charlotte, South Carolina to his home in Florida.

That 600-mile trip to his plush new $11 million dollar mansion in Palm Beach Gardens, next to the Jack Nicklaus owned 'Bear Club Golf Club', takes 10 hours by car or two hours flying. He revealed:

Something that people don't know is that I went back home. Everyone was talking about how I showed back about half an hour before my tee time on the last day. I actually had a nap and my dad had to come and wake me up because I overslept. He said to me: 'Rory, you realise you have to play golf this afternoon.' I didn't know where I was!

Those shaves were really too close for comfort but the buck really stops with 'Ollie'. How a Ryder Cup Captain, who held such an emotive meeting with his team the night before, could allow this was baffling.

A Ryder Cup Captain should always have his team assembled at all times. It is after all only three days every two years. Players support each other when not playing so they should be assembled together on the morning of play.

Colin Montgomerie should really have directed his comments at Olazabal and the Vice Captains when, on hearing about McIlroy's late arrival, 'Monty' told a reporter: 'That is quite ridiculous at this level. It's quite unbelievable for the world number one.'

****

Luke Donald may have been Europe's first player on the tee in the final days play, but it was the second man out, Paul Lawrie, who got Europe off to the perfect start and won them their first point. The Scot thumped Brandt Snedeker 5 and 3.

He was 4-up on the American with four holes left to play and he won it at the 15th to be 5-up with just three holes left. It was also his second singles win from two played after hammering Jeff Maggert 4 and 3 in 1999 where he also enjoyed a foursomes and fourball win with Monty.

Donald held off Bubba Watson 2 and 1 to secure Europe's second point in a row. The score was 10-8 and Europe were right back in it. But there were still a lot of matches out on the course that were too close to call, which meant the US still held a big advantage.

Two games were done and dusted and all eyes now turned to Rory versus Keegan Bradley. The two 'Irishmen' had contrasting fortunes over the previous two days. Keegan won three out of three points. Rory won two and lost two .

There was nothing to separate them past the halfway stage but Bradley was just not in the same form as previously. It was noticeable that he was struggling very badly with his irons.

Rory won back-to-back holes on 13 and 14 to go 2-up and the Northern Irishman finished the tie on the par-three 17th hole with a par. Incredibly the Europeans were now just a point behind trailing 10-9.

Attention now turned to 'Mr Ryder Cup', as some were now calling him. Ian Poulter was at it again. He was involved in a titanic duel with former US Open champ Webb Simpson and as only to be expected, it went right to the wire.

However, as he shook hands with Simpson earlier that day to begin 'Match Number Four', he had to endure more taunts from the crowds again. Let Paul Hayward of the London Telegraph describe his walk to the first tee:

The Chicago crowd knew how to taunt Ian Poulter. 'Major winner, major winner', they chanted, as Webb Simpson, America's US Open champion arrived on the first tee for their singles match. They mocked Poulter's record in the big four stroke-play events as there was no mud they could throw at him with regard to Ryder Cups.

The American responded to the crowds urgings and was 2-up through six holes. Then another taunt cried out: 'Hey Ian, where are your coloured shoes?'

But what the crowds failed to realise was that they were only fuelling his fire. They may have felt that they had a new 'Colin Montgomerie' to target, a new 'Mrs Doubtfire', and so they just could not contain themselves.

Poulter blotted it all out and he just focussed on the job against Simpson. So much so that when he birdied the 14th, he refused to concede the American's five-foot birdie attempt on the same hole.

Incredibly, Ian Poulter, who went on a birdie blitz with Rory the previous day to haul Europe back from the brink of near certain defeat, then repeated the dose. Lightning struck the same bolt twice.

Unbelievably he birdied 14, then 15 and 16 to draw level, and then he won the 17th to take the lead and the 18th to close out a 2-up victory. Five birdies in a row! The Europeans on the side lines lifted him in the air.

With Europe now level at 10-10, Jose Maria Olazabal declared: 'I think the Ryder Cup should build a statue to him!'

The Americans were shell shocked and the Europeans were ecstatic. The team talk the night before was working. Could the unimaginable happen? Could Europe win? Were the Yanks bottling it?

Sheer bliss and joy abounded and rebounded throughout Camp Europe. Then the wise and sensible ones shushed the excited ones. And as if to show that chickens were not to be counted in advance, Dustin Johnson dampened and poured water on the great hopes.

With clubs looking like small wands in his hand, his magic was too good for another big hitter that day. He beat Nicolas Colsaerts 3 and 2. United States regained the lead again as concerned faces looked up at the scores of those remaining out there.

It was looking good for the US. Despite the great European comeback, America held a slim 11-10 lead after winning match number six with five matches completed. Europe had no comfortable lead in the other seven except for Lee Westwood who was 3-up on Kuchar.

In the fifth game ongoing, Mickelson was 1-up on Rose after 16 and it was very tight in the remainder involving Zach Johnson and McDowell, Garcia and Furyk, Dufner and Hanson, Stricker and Kaymer and the last match out, Woods and Molinari.

Phil Mickelson had two holes to play and if he hung on to win then America would need just two more wins and a half, or one win and three halves, to lift the Cup. It was looking good.

It was a humdinger of a battle between both and the following year they would be at it again in the US Open. The Englishman birdied from 20 feet on the first and also won the second after Mickelson found water.

The American coolly fought back to square the match only for Rose to eagle the seventh after a marvellous shot finished eight feet from the pin. 'Lefty' then won the eighth but was soon 1-down again at the ninth.

Rose failed to save par on the 11th and a great escape from a bunker on the 14th put Mickelson 1-up. On the 16th Rose sank a very important putt to deny his opponent a 2-up lead. Then a burst of drama arrived.

On the putting surface at 17, Justin Rose had a huge breaking putt fully the length of the green. He would do well to get down in two for par. It moseyed in the hole! Europe were level – a shocked Mickelson, to his credit, applauded the effort.

Both players found good drives off the tee at the final hole but Mickelson over-clubbed and found the light rough with his approach. Rose hit another great shot to 12 feet for a possible birdie.

Phil could still chip in for birdie but on this occasion he had to settle for par. Rose got down and surveyed his putt; he had to make it to win. He drained it right in the middle. Quite incredibly, Europe had turned this one around as well. The score was 11-11!

A beaming Rose, mobbed by his team and supporters, said as he came off the green: 'I wouldn't say I've made three bigger putts back-to-back in my career ever.'

Back out on the course though, Graeme McDowell was still struggling with his game. He was just hanging on to the shirt tail of Zach Johnson and eventually lost 2 and 1. 12-11 to the United States and it was another bad blow that stopped the European momentum again.

Europe had fought valiantly only for two results to come up and whack them in the jaw. It was difficult to stomach after they had moved heaven and earth. But that was always going to be the scenario from 11.03 that morning – up against it.

Trailing 10-6 means the US were always in sight of victory. It was therefore very timely when Westwood got his game over and easily beat Kuchar 3 and 2. The scores were level again at 12-12. Clenched fists and a 'YESSSS' sigh of relief all around Europe.

Only four matches were left out on the course and Europe needed one last miracle from the position they were in. None of the games were going their way and United States must have been 1/100 on with bookmakers to win the Cup.

Peter Hanson was losing heavily to Dufner; Garcia was losing to Furyk and the remaining two ties involving Stricker/Kaymer and Woods/Molinari were deadlocked. All the prayers to Seve and the team talk had worked – but one last surge was needed.

In the 'spirit' of Seve and 'captained' by Ollie the script could not have been written any better, and 'played' out by the only Spanish player. Sergio Garcia, more than any other, turned the tide.

Cometh the hour, cometh the man and at the last gasp moment,

Sergio surged. It really has to be said though, that his opponent Jim Furyk fell apart from being in a commanding position.

There was nothing between both players all day. Furyk went 1-up at the 12th only for Sergio to level at the next before the unassuming, quiet American regained the lead. But with just 17 and 18 left, he blew up.

He missed the putting surface with his nine iron on the par-three 17th and so missed his par putt from 10 feet. Garcia secured par to level. It got even worse for Furyk and the hundreds of millions of Americans watching worldwide.

With a short five-foot putt on the 18th to shake hands on a fair draw, he missed! Without doing anything really spectacular on the last two holes, Garcia was gifted the win by a distraught Furyk. The Spaniard was ecstatic.

Europe led again 13-12 but not for long. Moments later Jason Dufner put paid to Peter Hanson. The Swede battled hard over the last few holes but 'The Duff' was probably America's best player that day. He was 4-up through eight and won 2-up.

13-13! There were just four golfers out on the course and this most gripping of all Ryder Cup encounters – the greatest of all time – was deadlocked. Twenty six points had been shared equally and each of the other two matches were 'all square' entering the final holes.

Just one point was needed for Europe to retain the Cup. So even if both rubbers finished the way they were and all square, 14-14 would be enough. Because of that scenario they had to play on, because America, in their own backyard, needed the win.

One point for the United States and a half in the other would mean an American win. Of course two to nil would be even sweeter after the humiliation and indignity of having to endure such a backlash and onslaught from Europe.

Two-nil to Europe would mean the greatest comeback in history without any doubt. So many different scenarios could result from just two games and it was gripping, riveting and fingernail-biting stuff!

How did those last four players stand still or swing their clubs properly? Snooker players making a clearance to win a world title, or achieving a 147, have testified to feeling their hearts beating loudly in their ears as they tried to prevent their cue arm shaking.

Their success is achieved in the silence of an arena – this was pure circus, pandemonium and bedlam. So how must Martin Kaymer and Steve Stricker have felt and coped when they saw the multitudes moving towards and homing in on them!

Germany's Martin Kaymer, the man who was in such poor form when the team was announced a year before, that rumours abounded he was going to turn down the offer. He was going to do what Sandy Lyle had done and pull out of the Ryder Cup.

Kaymer went to see Bernhard Langer on Friday to consult his fellow German about his poor form. Perhaps that is why he was only allotted one game before the singles and in that Friday fourball he and Justin Rose lost.

Now all eyes were transfixed on him. In a dour battle with Steve Stricker, Kaymer went 1-up at the ninth but Stricker squared it at the 15th. Then there was more drama as Stricker bogeyed the penultimate hole.

The German teed off on the 18th knowing that if he could maintain his 1-up lead for a few more minutes, he and Europe would win. He teed off and put his ball in a fairway bunker. But the American made a mess of things as well.

Perhaps the crowds circling around the pair had caused this. It got messy – very messy. Kaymer was soon in a brilliant position to win after playing a great shot from the bunker to the green.

He had two shots for the win but he played a very poor putt up the green to the pin and was left with a nasty eight-footer. Sink that three meter putt Martin Kaymer and you will go down in history as the man who won the 2012 Ryder Cup.

After his meeting with Langer on Friday, how tragically ironic it would be if he missed as Langer had done in 1991 (handing the US victory). Kaymer admitted later that he had thought about his compatriot's famous miss as he lined it up. He said:

I did think about it – especially when I went around and read the putt from the other side. So I thought, 'ok, it's not going to happen again, IT IS NOT GOING TO HAPPEN AGAIN'.

What massive pressure to endure. And in that moment, for one of golf's genuine nice guys, you did not want him to miss. He did not. He coolly hit the ball straight in the middle. Europe 14; US 13 meant they had retained the Cup.

The 'Charge of the Light Brigade' ensued. Garcia leapt on top of him. It was without any doubt the most amazing comeback – much more so than Brookline. This had been miraculously achieved. Kaymer said:

My brother was here, my father was here, and then Sergio Garcia ran on to the green. It means so much more when they are all standing behind me. Now I know how it really feels to win a Ryder Cup.

Strictly speaking it was actually Molinari back on the 18th who 'won' the match for Europe while Kaymer sank the putt that 'retained' and therefore won the Ryder Cup. Molinari's half point actually caused consternation and controversy back in the States.

Tiger Woods was severely criticised and questioned over his decision to call a halt to proceedings and settle for a draw with the Italian. He said:

It was already over. The Cup had already been retained by Europe. It's pointless to even finish. So 18 was just 'hey, get this over with'.

'USA Today' said about Woods: 'Not only a man the USA couldn't rely on, he was a player who at times appeared to be barely here.'

Rory McIlroy had been a part of the greatest Ryder Cup in history. What sets this one apart from the other great comebacks was the great sportsmanship – highlighted by Davis Love's generous tribute to Seve.

The only negativity was some of the taunting emanating from certain elements of the crowd – something European crowds do not engage in. But nothing could take away from a truly remarkable event.

Something 'freaky' and 'weird' really did happen. Near the end, after a five to nothing start, Europe looked dead and buried, with any loss in four close ties enough to end their cause. There had to be something else to explain all this. Was it paranormal? Was it 'Divine

Intervention'?

The only other modern sporting sensation that it could be likened to was Italian jockey Frankie Dettori's stunning seven winners from the seven race card at Ascot in 1996, which was euphemistically termed, 'Frankie's Magnificent Seven'.

It was unprecedented. With world class jockeys, world class horses and big fields of 20 or more runners, it had never been done before and it will never be achieved again. Frankie has since put it down to divine intervention.

Here is what some of the winning team had to say. What they stated may just give us a tiny flavour of the incredible feeling that they experienced not just on the day and in the heat of battle, but more especially in the team meeting the previous night.

I felt something in that team room last night that was incredible [getting emotional]. They did it to us in '99 [US win from 10-6 down in Brookline] and it's up to the guys out there now but if we can do it, it will be the most incredible comeback of all time. [Ian Poulter immediately after his win]

I've never cried as many tears as I cried last night. There were tears everywhere. [Paul Lawrie]

I am just so proud of my partners. And [gets emotional] there is no doubt Seve was looking down on us because some of the breaks I got out there today were incredible. [Sergio Garcia]

Let Rory McIlroy have the last word. The young man capped off a sensational year with another fabulous personal performance. After two points from four in the 2010 event, he accumulated three points from five here.

He did that without McDowell firing fully on all cylinders; he played in every one of the five sessions and he had to contend with a rushed, very late to the tee start, on the final day. His words sum up and echo everything that has been said already:

He [Ollie], has made us all cry in the team room this week. Some of us were in tears in there. Seve was looking down on us and it has all been one of the most incredible moments that I've ever experienced on a golf course.

You know, they say if you wish to have someone canonised a Saint, that you must first approach your priest or bishop with evidence of a miracle. This will then be documented and sent to the powers that be in the Vatican for their consideration.

I do not know if there are many Saints that have emanated from the world of sport. What I do know is that there have been many sports competitors who have done more for the poor and ordinary working class people throughout the world than many Saints.

Saint Severiano? There is evidence of a miracle at Medinah which people throughout the world marvelled and wondered at. It touched the lives of countless millions of men, women and children of all ages and religions.

Among them were the poor, sick, dying and working class; kings, queens, presidents and prime ministers as well as priests, nuns and cardinals; millionaires, billionaires and upper class.

Facilitated by a Captain, Vice Captain and their 12 Disciples but ultimately.... All spellbound by the spirit of Seve.

Chapter 8

THE DOLDRUMS

In January 2013, Rory McIlroy officially became a global sports superstar. Of course he had been a superstar of golf for the previous few years. That was before he signed up as a stable mate of Tiger Woods at sports merchandise giant, Nike.

On Monday 14 January, Rory appeared at one of those specially convened conferences in front of a select audience. Reminiscent of Bill Gates and Microsoft, Cindy Davis (the President of Nike Golf) and Rory sat on stools across from each other.

She was there to announce the worst kept secret that to be doing the rounds since the end of the previous year: that Nike had signed up Rory and he would be using specially made Nike clubs from that day forward. It was out with his trusted clubs, in with the new.

With brand Nike and brand Rory now amalgamating, at that very moment he became one of the most famous and instantly recognisable faces on the planet. Nike would do with Rory what they had achieved with Tiger Woods – or so that was their best laid plans.

If both parties thought it was going to be an easy ride, that the mega bucks from worldwide sales of Nike products would flow in like petrodollars, then they were in for a very rude awakening.

From the start there were doubters with former golfers – and sports stars who use equipment – quick to point out the pitfalls and dangers of suddenly reverting to pristine new products. Foremost among them was Sir Nick Faldo. He stated:

I call it dangerous. I've changed clubs and changed equipment, and every manufacturer will say, 'We can copy your clubs, we can tweak the golf ball so it fits you'. But there's feel and sound as well as confidence. You can't put a real value on that.

Over the following months Faldo was asked to clarify and elaborate on these points, to which Rory, obviously getting a little terse at these constant remarks, not to mention the fact he was practicing hard and long hours with the clubs, replied: 'Nick Faldo doesn't know how I feel over the ball.'

Rory first tried out his new clubs in late November the previous year. The day after he shot a -6, 66 (with his old Titleist clubs) to trail Luke Donald by a shot in the World Tour Championship, he gave an initial reaction to them when he divulged:

After the Ryder Cup I started to test a little bit but I've six or seven weeks to really get into it though I'm pretty much set with everything. It's just a matter of getting confidence and playing a few rounds and I should be ok.

I'm very confident they [Nike's manufacturers] will get it spot on. I've got a set of irons and the woods sorted and it's just a matter of getting the ball dialed in. It's the feel of the ball that I find is the most important thing because really, every manufacturer makes great equipment these days.

Former American golden boy golfer Johnny Miller was another man to question Rory's decision, but he did have many followers who saw no problem with his switch. Fellow European golfer Paul Casey gave him a firm vote of confidence saying:

When I first came on tour 10 years ago, there wasn't the information there is now to fit golf clubs and to interpret what clubs and balls do. Tools like 'Trackman' and a lot of biomechanics stuff can tell a player he's swinging the same way and changes are not the players fault. Nike staff do this sort of thing day in, day out. They make it pretty damn easy. As well as that, this is the world's best golfer and he's pretty good at the game.

Also on the plus side was a precedent set by Graeme McDowell.

In 2010 he switched clubs after he won the US Open. He began his next season with the new clubs in a tournament in Hawaii where he shot a first round 62.

On 17 January, three days after his appearance with Nike, Rory teed off at the Abu Dhabi Championship in Dubai. For the first time in professional competition, he used their clubs and merchandise.

He came home with a poor first Round 75. He followed that with another 75 the next day to miss the cut. It was not a great start to his new relationship with Nike but it was put down to teething problems and trying to get to grips with the new equipment.

A month later at the Accenture World Matchplay, Rory was confronted with snowballs! Snow hit the Arizona Desert and forced a complete wipeout of play on Wednesday and further delays on the Thursday.

Before his match got underway, he was pelted with snowballs by his fellow Irishman and opponent Shane Lowry. The Offaly man then went on to sensationally knock him out in the first round by beating him on the final hole.

Rory lost 1-down; he could so easily have been 4-up through the first four holes but failed to take his chances. After that his iron play deserted him with one infamous moment coming at the 10th where his ball ended up 20 yards short of the green from just 130 yards away.

Having reached the final the previous year, such was his miserable run in 2013 that the first round exit came as no surprise. Afterwards Rory said that if he had played anyone else rather than playing Lowry in an atmosphere of joviality, he would have been hammered.

On the state of his game, he gave these views:

I was missing a lot of irons. I felt like I drew the ball really well and I hit it well off the tee. I just need to take advantage of the driving I have been doing. It is more a timing thing than anything else. Everything else was actually pretty good out there. I just need to go and work on them [my iron play].

It never rains but it pours and much worse was to follow when Rory did an unbelievable thing which he later regretted and apologized for. At the Honda Classic on the last day of February, things seemed to be going ok when he shot a first round of level par 70.

Then without any warning, and midway through his second round next day, he walked off the golf course and out of the tournament! The world's media literally clambered over themselves to find out why.

Initially he told reporters that he was 'not mentally there'. Later he elaborated further to reveal that he had 'problem wisdom teeth that have been giving a lot of pain for some time.'

McIlroy then realized what he had done was wrong. Before the PGA powers that be settled down to discuss what action to take against him, Rory issued a heartfelt apology on the following Wednesday 6 March on the eve of the WGC Cadillac event. It read:

I realized pretty quickly it was not the right thing to do. At that moment in time I was all over the place and I just saw red. I feel like I let a lot of people down with what I did last week, and for that I am sorry.

No matter how bad I was playing, I should have stayed out there. I should have tried to shoot the best score possible even though it was not going to be enough for me to make the cut.

In the Cadillac, he opened with another very poor round of 73 but at least finished the event with an impressive 65 to finish in the top 10. If he thought it would be the catalyst for great things to come, then Rory had quite another think coming.

That 65 – his lowest round in four events using the new clubs – would actually end up being one of his lowest rounds of the season. Rory was not to know it then but it would only be bettered by one shot towards the end of his season.

The month of March also brought bad news in the World Rankings. Tiger Woods, back and as good as ever, though perhaps not in majors, replaced McIlroy as world number one after winning that Cadillac.

Woods would accumulate an amazing five wins that season which did not include his Tavistock Cup and Presidents Cup successes. He won January's Farmers Insurance, the Cadillac and Arnold Palmer in March, the Players in May and saved his best until last.

In August, he won the WGC Bridgestone Invitational but in doing so, he shot his lowest round for some years. In his second round he totaled 61 blows, nine under. He was true to his very words a year earlier when warning everyone he was getting better and better.

At the Shell Houston Open three weeks after the Cadillac, Rory failed to hit a single round in the 60s. Four rounds of 70+ meant he finished tied 45th. In poor form and in a desperate bid to get in more match practice, he took a very unusual step.

He decided to play just one week before the season's first major, the US Masters, at the unfashionable Valero Texas Open. He simply had to get in some good form ahead of Augusta.

His decision to head to Texas proved to be very worthwhile and fulfilling. After an unspectacular 72 start, he finished with 67, 71 and 66 to finish second. It was the ideal preparation for the Masters. He could now go there with form and confidence.

A wide smile came back to his face. He could now stand tall again. That is what confidence, and in particular a great result – any result, anywhere – does for the sports competitor. So much so that he made an announcement to the media.

After four months of playing and practicing with the new Nike golf clubs, he felt very comfortable with them. As far as he was concerned, he had sorted all issues with the clubs. And there were issues – as he was to point out at the British Open later.

Initially things went well for Rory in the season's opening major. Following early rounds of 72, 70 he was two under and had made the cut for the weekend. Then disaster struck him down again at the Augusta course as he shot 79 in the third round.

A final battling round of 69 was scant consolation for his final position of tied 25th. The bottom line was that he could not get the consistency he was normally accustomed to. He was hitting too many rounds without breaking 70.

That exact same scenario applied three weeks later when Rory ventured to his favourite Wells Fargo event at Quail Hollow. The beautiful feel good factor of the place inspired him to a lovely opening round of five under, 67.

Then the curse struck again with rounds of 71, 73 and 73 for a 10th place finish. The same applied again a week later at a course he struggles at – Sawgrass for the Players Championship. He opened with six under, 66 and ended 72, 73, and 70 for eighth place.

It was so frustrating. Any one of those rounds over par was costing him the chance of a first victory under his new sponsors. He was literally going around with 'one wheel on my wagon' as the song goes. Then all the wheels came off.

****

Rory McIlroy endured a torrid start to his new mega million dollar career with Nike. Using their new clubs to replace his trusted old ones from the start of 2013, his form was all over the place. It seemed as if he could not get to grips with them at all.

It was to get much worse before it got better. He flew back home to the UK after the Players Championship to play the prestigious BMW at Wentworth in Surrey. On this occasion he did not even make it to the weekend.

He missed the cut with rounds of 74 and 75 and then flew back across the Atlantic to play the Memorial Tournament in Ohio exactly one week later. He opened with a catastrophic 78.

Rory must have felt like not only tearing his hair out, but smashing up his new clubs as well. He was trying everything. Off the course (as he would later tell Nick Faldo), he was practicing from early morning until there were blisters on his hands in the evening.

Although he just about made the cut in the Memorial, things did not improve much and he finished tied 57th. A fortnight later the US Open arrived and he was going into the second major of the year on the back of some of the worst run of form in his professional career.

Rounds of 73, 70, 75 and a miserable last round 76 only tells you that Rory was now well and truly stuck in the doldrums. There was seemingly no way out of there. Even he must surely have had grave doubts about the new clubs at this stage.

It is only human nature. At the forefront of his mind, he would have had big block capital neon signs blinding him with their constant flashing of the message that he had never endured such a run as this with his old clubs.

Perhaps a trip back across the ocean to his homeland for the Irish Open on 27 June would do the trick. Nope – another missed cut ensued after rounds of 74, 72. Something had to happen and fast as the British Open was up next. It was becoming a real crisis.

After the Irish Open, Rory revealed that he was still working with Nike's equipment to find the perfect putter and driver. This was pounced upon once more by the man who felt Rory had made a mistake in getting rid of his old clubs.

Nick Faldo was sought out again for his opinions and he was not short of offering them. From newspapers to American television channels, Sir Nick was now in effect telling everybody 'I told you so'. He said:

Rory very simply messed with a winning formula. He went form rookie of the year to world number one and has been through a lot and thought he could start again. As I said from day one – I tweeted right away when it [the Nike deal] was announced – that this was a dangerous move. People said, 'Oh, he's so talented, he can adapt.' Well, why should the world number one be adapting to something new? As we discovered six months later, he's busy still trying putters, still trying drivers. It's not as easy.

Faldo elaborated further:

We get a millisecond of feel at impact and if it's going great then it builds confidence; if it's suddenly something different to what you've been doing, or think you're going to do, then that hurts your confidence. So I hope he hasn't gone too far but it has damaged his confidence.

Then in July just before the British Open, Faldo blamed Rory's poor form on so many things going on in his life off the course. He intimated that (apart from the new clubs) business deals and his taking time off to be with his girlfriend were affecting Rory.

The British player, who won six majors, went on to add that Rory should sacrifice everything and replace it with 'a 20 year window as an athlete of concentrating on nothing else but golf.' He added:

I actually think there's a lot going on in his mind… I always felt, as my career went on, I got involved in business and other things. Once your concentration goes, you need 100% concentration, off the golf course, practicing, as well. The most ideal thing is to go to the club at nine in the morning, hit balls all day long, and you leave at five pm.

Rory hit back with:

I saw what he said. He said I should be hitting balls from nine to five. Well, I was up at 6.15 this morning and in the gym until 6.45. That's a 12 hour day compared to his eight . It is what it is, and Nick should know how hard this game is at times. He's been in our position before. And he should know how much work that we all do put into it."

This squared almost exactly with a routine which Rory would later outline to a reporter who asked him what a typical day is like in his life. He replied:

I'm usually in the gym at seven and I'm in there for around one and a half hours. Then I get some breakfast and go to the course. I'll practice, hit a few balls and work on my short game from maybe 10 am – 1 pm. After lunch I'll then go out and play some holes – nine or 18 – and then some days I'm back in the gym from 5.30 – 7 pm. In the evening before going to bed, I sometimes read a little. I like the autobiographies of Agassi; Alex Ferguson and a book called 'Tales From the Secret Footballer'. Then it's lights out.

Before the British Open teed off, Rory gave a BBC on-course reporter an insight into one specific problem that he was having with the clubs. After adding a special 'pear shaped' Driver to his bag, he showed the reporter the club and revealed the reason for adding it:

"I've had a tendency off the tee to keep turning the ball off to the right and it ends up in the light rough or rough. So I've been practicing with this on the range and it seems to be working well. Hopefully it will put an end to the problem of hitting it out right."

In the first round of that 142nd Open at Muirfield, Rory shot a disastrous +8, 79. It was one of his poorest rounds ever in an Open. Nick Faldo also shot 79 and feeling that Rory had been offended by some of his remarks, he moved to clarify his comments:

I'm friends of Rory, don't write it any other way. I've known him since he was 12. He's a big part of my Faldo Series. I'm like big granddad here, saying exactly those things — 'Just give it your full attention, when you want to play golf, when you want to disappear and have a family and do other things.' I'm trying to give him a little loving, caring help here. I like the kid. He's a friend and I can speak from experience. All I'm trying to say is I've been there, seen it and I know what can happen.

He added:

As I said right from the word go, I thought the equipment change was very dangerous and tried to explain the feel factor and confidence. He looks like a different person, let alone a different golfer right now. When I saw him before the PGA last year, he said 'every part of my game is good'. He wouldn't say that now would he.

Following his terrible start, Rory did not know what to think anymore – literally. He was already 13 shots behind leader Zach Johnson and had a massive job to make the cut. As he faced the waiting ranks of media battalions, he looked perplexed as he explained:

That was brain dead. I don't know what you can do. You've just got to play your way through it. It's nothing to do with technique – it's all mental out there. I just need to concentrate as sometimes I feel like I'm walking around out there and I'm unconscious.

A 75 next day meant huge disappointment for Rory. In a major that he desperately wants to win, he failed to qualify for the final two rounds. Nike must have been hugely disappointed as well with regard to worldwide focus on the Open and his absence from it.

Rory at this stage had missed the cut in three successive and very prestigious European events together with some very poor showings in America. Worse than that, he had virtually been non existent in the first three majors of the year.

His next event at the Bridgestone Invitational on 1 August followed a similar pattern. More rounds of 70+ and a tied 27th finish. With the last major the USPGA just a week away, there were no positive signs of a recovery.

It looked very likely that, after a major win in 2011 and 2012, this was going to be an empty season in that regard. Just when things could not get any worse on the course, off course major controversies were brewing.

Rory's season of woe would continue. In particular, two colossal demons that now joined forces with the clubs issue to further confuse Rory and cause very worrying confrontations in his head.

Chapter 9

COURT v CLUB v COUNTRY

Quite apart from the issues over his new Nike clubs, another reason why Rory was 'brain dead', as well as being in such poor form, could have been the impending split with his management team of 18 months, Horizon.

Although their parting was made official in early September 2013, it was speculated upon for months in advance. The official statement from Horizon Sports Management came under banner newspaper headlines such as this:

'RORY MCILROY SPLIT WITH HORIZON LIKELY TO SPARK LEGAL BATTLE'

Their statement read as follows:

Since October 2011, Horizon has achieved exceptional results for Rory in realising his commercial objectives. Under Horizon's management, Rory has signed some of the most lucrative endorsements in sports history. The current contract has a number of years to run. Rory's decision to seek a termination of the management contract with Horizon is now regrettably in the hands of legal advisors.

Rory was now in a new management structure set up by his father Gerry. It was named, 'Rory McIlroy Incorporated' (RMI) with Donal Casey its Chief Executive Officer (CEO). He was an actuary by profession but had many years experience as a CEO.

Barry Funston, a business leader and long time friend of the McIlroy family would head up the 'Rory Foundation for Charity'. Both he and Gerry would also serve on the RMI Board.

Many may have seen this as a bit haphazard and very perilous. But it was becoming part of a modern trend. Australian golfer Adam Scott had set up his own management company headed by his father Phil, and in 2014 Graeme McDowell would leave Horizon.

However, Rory's new set up and strong family influences might have seemed all very stable, secure and comfortable to him on the outside. But underneath, the threat of legal action can have a very unsettling affect.

That is particularly so if it drags on and is not resolved. There were stories that both sides were content to go all the way to the High Court in Dublin and that the case would be scheduled for November 2014.

A second monster plaguing Rory was the question of who he would represent in the 2016 Brazil Olympics – Team GB or Ireland. This issue really stressed Rory and we had no idea how much until Graeme McDowell lifted the lid on the matter some time later.

Rory said consistently that he had not made a decision and would not make one until nearer the 2016 Olympics. With all the constant press speculation mounting, in September 2012 Rory said:

Whatever I do, I know my decision is going to upset some people but I just hope the best majority will understand. What makes it such an awful position to be in is that I've grown up my whole life playing for the Golfing Union of Ireland. But the fact is I've always felt more British than Irish. Maybe it's the way I was brought up, I don't know. But I've always felt more of a connection with the UK than with Ireland. And so I have to weigh that up with having played for Ireland so it is tough.

All sorts of people from sports stars to televison stars had an opinion on the matter. Even Rory's ex girlfriend Holly Sweeney weighed in with: 'He always made it clear to me [that he was British]'.

Rory made another statement on 10 September 2012 which read:

I am a proud product of Irish golf. I'm also a proud Ulsterman who grew up in Northern Ireland. I've absolutely not made a decision regarding my participation in the Olympics.

So I decided to try to do something about all of this. I could see even more pitfalls ahead for Rory. Unknownst to himself, he could have been digging even bigger holes to fall into.

For instance, one thing that was not discussed and taken into greater consideration by Rory – or the media – was the feelings of golfers probably more deserving of a Team GB Olympic spot.

Those that have represented England, Scotland and Wales over the years in World Cups. What were their feelings on this, and could friendships with Rory be put in jeopardy as a result of Rory, in some people's eyes, getting a little too far ahead of himself?

What were the feelings of Paul Lawrie; Paul Casey; Lee Westwood; Ian Poulter; Luke Donald; Ross Fisher; Stephen Gallacher; Martin Laird and Jamie Donaldson as well as many other potential candidates for just a few Olympic spots?

After all, there is a well known photo of Rory and Graeme McDowell attired in smart suits walking behind the Irish Tricolor at a World Cup. Rory actually represented Ireland several times at this event.

That is not to mention the scores of times he represented Ireland and the GUI at Boys and Youths Internationals as well as Home Internationals over the years. So some of the top British golfers might start to question how, all of a sudden, could he represent Team GB?

On the weekend of 5 October, I contacted Pat Hickey of the Olympic Council of Ireland. I asked him if he felt Rory McIlroy, who has walked behind the Tricolor at past World Cups, could perhaps be Ireland's flagbearer in Rio, 2016. Pat replied emphatically:

Absolutely. I'll put it to you this way: If Rory McIlroy declares for Ireland, then he will automatically put himself in pole position to carry the Irish flag in Rio for the 2016 Brazil Olympics.

Then I talked with Adam Sills in London. Adam is Sports Editor of The Telegraph. He liked the idea as a major story and so, on Tuesday

9 October 2012, it appeared in their sports supplement as well as on the front page of the Irish Independent.

Many of the world's top sports have carried their country's flags at the opening ceremony of an Olympics. People like Roger Federer (Switzerland) and Maria Sharapova (Russia's first female flagbearer) to name but a few.

I knew that when the story broke, Rory would get to hear about it. When he did, he would have food for thought. It could also be something that might just stir or awaken 'real' patriotic tendencies.

Quite aside from the choice he was referring to in the media, to be made before Rio 2016, this was an altogether more relaxed choice. On the one hand you had a loaded explosive choice and on the other you had a potentially nice, thrilling one to mull over.

The flag choice basically boiled down to this:

(i)   Do I declare for Ireland with whom I've played and have the chance to carry the Tricolor in Rio?

(ii) Do I declare for Team GB for whom I've never played and with very little chance of ever carrying the Union Jack?

While Rory mulled over that, Graeme McDowell had a new partner for Ireland at the 2013 World Cup of Golf in Melbourne, Australia. Rory withdrew because of all the furore.

Despite the fact that he had walked with McDowell directly behind a Tricolor in the 2009 and 2011 World Cups, he felt that representing Ireland this time would only compromise his position of consistently saying that he would not made a decision until nearer to Rio.

Graeme McDowell remained hopeful that McIlroy would join him in Australia.

I need my partner in crime in Melbourne and regardless whether Rory wants to play or not, I want to play this year. If it works, I'd like him to be there, as well. But we'll see.

As referred to earlier, G-Mac would later make a heartfelt plea to

Olympic authorites. He stated that after talking with Rory at length about the matter, Rory was worried and stressed out over the whole saga.

He therefore asked that the decision be made for him. Europe's 2014 Ryder Cup captain Paul McGinley weighed in on the argument. He agreed with McDowell. He also suggested that there was a strong possibility Rory would not go to the Olympics.

McGinley said:

All I can say is that unless something is done, I really don't think Rory will play in the Olympics which would be a shame – not just for the world of golf but for the Olympics as well.

He continued:

I'm one of those people who doesn't think sport and politics mix and we can all see that Rory has a real problem here. I agree with Graeme McDowell who said that someone from the International Olympic Committee or a similar body should come forward and make the decision for him. As things stand, Rory is being asked to offend someone and that's not right. He is not that sort of guy. He shouldn't be placed in that situation.

This is a flavour of how I dealt with this controversial topic in the last book in 2011:

By far and away the biggest controversy of his career so far, is one that is set to be continually played out for many decades to come. It is the question of his, shall we say, 'patriotic allegiance'.

Renowned golf journalist Charlie Mulqueen of Irish newspaper, The Examiner gives the intro to it:

There have been times when I wished Rory McIlroy had taken time to formulate an answer before expressing a view on anything that might be regarded as controversial. The remark, for instance, that he 'looked forward to being a member of Team UK' after it was announced that golf would be part of the Olympic Games rankled with many – and not just those with nationalistic leanings or the members of the GUI who had helped him along the way in his amateur days.

In The Telegraph of 29 September 2009, Mark Reason tried to make sense of it all as he explained and elaborated:

If you are McIlroy or Tommy Bowe and golf and rugby union are accepted into the 2016 Olympics at next week's vote of the International Olympic Committee, do you represent Great Britain or Ireland?

McIlroy told Telegraph Sport:

I'd probably play for Great Britain. I have a British passport. It's a bit of an awkward question still. It would be huge to play in an Olympics. I'd love to get an Olympic gold medal one day.

It is strange that golf and rugby should be up for inclusion at the same time because these are the sports that have historically unified Ireland. Ulster's rugby team come under the governance of the Irish Rugby Football Union and players from the north and the south turn out for one Ireland team. Golfers do the same. Formed in 1891 the Golfing Union of Ireland is the oldest golf union in the world and the presidency rotates between the four provinces. It does not matter if you hit your wedges in Ulster or Munster, you play amateur golf for Ireland.

Professional golf also recognises one Ireland. At November's World Cup in China there will not be a team from Northern Ireland and a team from the Republic, there will just be a team from Ireland. This year (2011) McIlroy and Graeme McDowell, both Ulster lads, will play for Ireland. Last year it was Graeme McDowell and Paul McGinley, who is from the south. On many previous occasions it has been McGinley and Padraig Harrington.

McDowell said after the International Olympic Commitee's

executive board proposed golf and rugby should be included in 2016 at a meeting last month:

It's a strange one. Golf's an all-Ireland sport. I'd play for anyone. I've never been able to explain why golf's an all-Ireland sport and rugby's an all-Ireland sport but soccer is two different teams. It'd be an honour to represent your country and I don't mind which one I play for, [...] it's the biggest sporting event on the planet. I'd love to be involved in it, love to win a gold medal. It's every young man's dream, huge for golf around the world. Golf needs to go to the masses. I'm not a fan of golf being an elitist sport. Fingers crossed I get a chance to do it.

Padraig Harrington said: 'In a country like Ireland, becoming an Olympic athlete is setting yourself apart. It is a major deal in Ireland. To be an athlete is an honour in itself.' But Harrington will not have to make a choice if golf makes it to the Olympics. McDowell and McIlroy will have to state an allegiance, like so many athletes from Northern Ireland have before them.

A few years ago, Eddie Irvine got in a quite undeserved bit of bother over what flag to hoist after he finished second in a Formula One race. Captain Peter McEvoy had a similar quandary at golf's 2001 Walker Cup. Someone had to hoist the tricolor at the opening ceremony but the two Irishmen in McEvoy's team, McDowell and Michael Hoey, were both from the north. McEvoy says:

In the end it didn't prove a problem and Michael was happy to do it as the amateur champion, but it could have been. It is strange that something like the Olympics comes along under the banner of good and we are now faced with this potential problem. It feels a bit of a retrograde step.

Peter Dawson, the chief executive of golf's governing body, the R&A, said: 'It's a question that has yet to be resolved, but I suspect that giving the players the choice is the likely outcome.'

As it transpired further down the line, nobody was going to make the decision for Rory or take it out of his hands. Despite what Peter Dawson said, Rory would have to make that choice himself.

When Graeme McDowell flew to Australia to represent Ireland again, he made his bed. He was making a firm statement that he would be honoured to play for Ireland in Rio 2016 if he was to be selected. The same was true of his new partner Shane Lowry.

Three time major winner Padraig Harrington was not to be forgotten. He was not only still banging on the majors door and telling all and sundry that he could still win another one, he was also openly stating that he would love to play for Ireland in Brazil.

McIlroy had yet to make any decision. In fact, as Paul McGinley had said, there were now very real dangers that he would not play in the Olympics at all.

But Rory would surprise all by coming to a decision much sooner than he had envisaged.

Chapter 10

WALTZING AUSTRALIA

Rory McIlroy was enduring a torrid 2013. Both on and off the course, nothing seemed to be going right. His game was in the doldrums and it was undoubtedly the worst run of form in his professional golf career.

What made the nightmare even more excruciating – and embarrassing – was that it just so happened to coincide with his mega-million dollar deal and switch to playing with Nike golf clubs. Off the course, things were even worse.

There were threats of legal action resulting from his leaving Horizon; every week there were headlines about whether he would play for Ireland or Team GB in the 2016 Olympic Games and even in his private life, malicious rumours were abound.

Despite the fact that, in between all the turmoil and heartache of under-performing, he got great solace and joy from being with his girlfriend Caroline Wozniacki, media speculation began to mount that the couple were breaking up.

It eventually petered out, especially since there were no friends or family on any one particular side who came forward to confirm it. In fact, both Rory and Caroline had to constantly deny the rumours.

The media were eventually sent whining and whimpering away with their tails between their legs, because in the weeks and months thereafter there was no more substance to the story. In the meantime Rory kept on hoping that somehow he could turn his form around.

After all the misery of missed cuts and down-the-field finishes, he was now heading to his favourite major, the USPGA. Not only had he gone close to winning this major the first few times he played in it, he was now going there as defending champion.

Everything seemed to be in his favour when thunderstorms drenched the course on the night before the event. As mentioned before, Rory is a class horse who goes on any ground but he has a real liking for soft ground conditions.

Played at Oak Hill in Rochester, New York, Rory could not have wished for a better start. He was three under through his first four holes but again he suffered a few wobbles. After the turn he suffered back-to-back bogeys on 10 and 11 before an electric storm saved him.

Lightning in the skies forced play to be suspended for over an hour and this gave Rory the chance to compose himself. He could talk to his coach Michael Bannon and the pair could iron out the reasons he made those bogeys to fall from three under to one under par.

It certainly had the desired effect as immediately on the resumption of play, he birdied the 12th with an eight-foot putt. But he then proceeded to bogey the 17th when taking three putts to get down.

On the 18th he also struggled but managed to make par when another bogey looked likely. His problems had not gone away and he had a lot of work to do. Still, a -1, 69 was a good start. It left him four shots behind both Adam Scott and Jim Furyk who carded 65's.

While American Jason Dufner ran amok in the second round with a marvellous seven under for 63, Rory's frustrations continued. This time he shot a one over round of 71 to find himself nine shots behind Dufner who held a two shot lead over Furyk, Scott and Matt Kuchar.

The story of Rory's third round is one of battling and brilliance. When he really had to shoot a very low score to cut the lead held by those at the top, he had to be content with a round that only got him back into contention, and no more.

However, a -3, 67 did give him a chance going into the final round. That was because those in front of him actually experienced contrasting fortunes, but the leading score remained at nine under par.

Jim Furyk showed his usual rock solid play and with rounds of 65, 68, and 68 he led by a shot from Dufner. But at least McIlroy moved forward after the likes of Justin Rose (with sevon over) and Kuchar (with six over) had days to forget.

So there was a certain satisfaction but it could have been an entirely different McIlroy mood had it not been for some of his magic on the last hole. Off the tee, Rory's ball swung 20 yards off course and over the heads of the crowds into deep rough.

When he arrived on the scene, it was a case of all hands on deck. Rory rolled up his sleeves while the crowds moved their portable chairs, bags and even the litter bins in order to clear a path for Rory.

With a four iron in hand he whacked the ball out and up towards the green, but it fell short and into more rough. His two under round was unravelling and he faced another -1, 69 or worse.

As he walked up the 18th fairway acknowledging the crowd, he must have been thinking about just what he had to do to get rid of the demons plaguing his game. Then, with a wedge, he chipped it in the hole for birdie as the crowd whooped it up with delight.

Six shots adrift overnight was no forlorn hope. Dufner had posted a 63 the previous day and similarly, if Rory could manage to pull out one big round, just as a poker player calls on that one big card, Rory could so easily post a similar score or better.

After his 67 he said:

I wouldn't say it was my best ball-striking round by any means but I got it up and down when I needed to. I knew they were going to toughen up the course. I sort of thought two 65s would have a chance, to 10 under par. I felt good enough about my game that I would go out there and post a good one to at least give myself a chance going into tomorrow.

So if he wanted to hit a 65 in both of the last two rounds, then by his calculations of 10 under, Rory now had to shoot 63 or better to be right in the thick of it. It was possible but in reality it was a tall order, and so it proved.

He shot a steady round of level-par 70 to remain three under. It was his highest finish since the Players Championship three months earlier when he also finished eighth. Jason Dufner on -10 fully deserved to win his first major by holding off Furyk by two shots.

A three week break ensued until he played again. The Barclays is an event that always signals a hectic end to the year. It is the first of the four Fedex Cup tournaments by the end of which one lucky golfer walks away with a cool $10 million bonus cheque.

Kevin Stadler, the son of legendary American golfer Craig 'The Walrus' Stadler, shot a stunning -7, 64 to lead after round one. Yet again Rory endured a topsy-turvy round eventually having to settle for an even par, 71.

Next day he shot 65 which was one of the best rounds he had put together for some considerable time. However, Matt Kuchar was now out on his own after he fired a double volley of 66, 65 to lead on -11.

As McIlroy had said in his last tournament, he now needed to blast two rounds of 65 to be in with a slim chance of winning this one. It never materialized. Another disappointing 71 effectively put paid to his chances as Kuchar on -12 was joined by Gary Woodland.

Among the middle starters in the final round, Rory never got anything going and finished on +1, 72. Adam Scott won a thrilling event by posting a 66. On -11, it was good enough to win by a shot from a group including Tiger Woods who tied second.

Rory tied 19th and although he was not out of the Fedex running, his hopes really vanished at the Deutsche Bank the following week. He ended in a share of 47th but one very positive thing did emanate from it.

In almost 10 months of competitive golf, he shot his lowest score of the year a 64. Coming off the back of a 65 the previous week and a 67 at the USPGA, this was most encouraging.

One round was not enough though. He needed the consistency of doing it over three or four rounds to emerge as a winner again. Nevertheless, shooting such a low round was evidence that the tide might be turning in his favour.

It got worse and a fortnight later at the BMW, it was almost a case of two steps forward, six steps back. He must have felt like packing in his golf for the rest of the season after recording a miserable 78 in the first round.

Contracts and commitments meant that there was no way he could ever do that and the ignominy did not end there. His season was summed up in the fact that finishing tied 57th meant he failed to qualify for the Fedex Cup's final event.

Not being part of the Tour Championship in Atlanta and the select group of 30 players battling for Fedex glory must have hurt him deeply. His game was now in crisis and even he, at that stage, must have started to feel that switching to Nike clubs had jinxed him.

Newspaper stories circulated to the effect that Rory was having sessions with leading sports psychologists. But the best psychology of all was to get out on the practice range and putting greens.

Doubtless he spent many hours meticulously doing just that with his coach as well as going through video footage, because he now had valuable time to do it. Missing the Fedex final meant that he had almost a month and a half until his next event.

'Things can only get better' as the lyrics go but Rory had been waiting a long time for his luck to change. He would also have another very long wait until his next event but perhaps a trip to the Far East might have a stimulating and refreshing effect.

****

Suitcases were packed and at the ready for a fairly long stint of activity involving tournaments in China, Saudi Arabia and Australia. Those destinations would be crammed into a hectic traveling schedule leading up to Christmas.

The events were spaced out fortnightly meaning Rory would jet off to an event in the East for one week and then jet back West. He would need at least a week to recover from the long haul flights and time differences.

First up was the HSBC event in Shezhan, Shanghai, which has not been kind to Rory over the years. Inaugurated in 2005, Phil Mickelson has won it twice along with the likes of Martin Kaymer and Ian Poulter.

After the monotony of the US Tour the sights and smells of this bustling Oriental City certainly helped. The weeks and weeks of hard work and preparation with his coach did not go to waste.

Rory opened up with an impressive 65. At seven under he was two shots ahead of Welshman Jamie Donaldson and Spaniard Gonzalo Fernandez Castano. But once again, old habits die hard and next day the gremlins returned to haunt him.

An even-par 72 in the second round ruined all chance he had

of winning the event because Dustin Johnson shot a brilliant nine under round of 63. That put him at the top on -12 and he never looked back after.

Two more excellent closing rounds of 66 and 66 gave the big American hitter a three shot winning margin over Ian Poulter with Graeme McDowell third. McIlroy's opening round was really what gave him a sixth place finish but he was all of nine shots behind Johnson.

A very interesting thing happened in China with a glowing tribute paid to Rory by Tiger Woods. He had seen Rory's game up close and personal from playing with him and out of the blue he blurted out to the world's media:

"Mark my words – Rory will win before the year is out."

Rory's frustrating form continued at the DP World Championship in Dubai two weeks later. Mediocre rounds were sandwiched between two very good rounds of 67 but once more there were signs he was making real progress.

After a sixth place in China, he finished fifth in the Middle East but the encouraging signs were to be seen in the fact that he shot two 67s. Incredibly it was his first time to do this since way back in April when rounds of 67 and 66 earned him a second placing in Texas.

The hard work seemed to be paying off. He had staved off bad results and now had two top 10 finishes in succession. Now the big question was, could he keep the consistency going to the point of going all the way to the winning post?

Sydney, Australia, was the third and final leg of the journey before Rory could rest up with family for Christmas. Australian golf officials had made several advances to Rory in the preceding years trying to get him to play their best tournaments.

However, Rory's schedule in the US, Europe and around the world meant that he could never get a chance to play in Australia. In actual fact this would only be his second trip Down Under, his first for six years.

In 2007, as a young scrawny teenager with a mop of curly black hair, he played in the Australian Masters in Melbourne, just his fifth tournament as a professional. He had turned pro in September and, from just four events played, he had amassed €277,000.

This amount secured his tour card for the 2008 European Tour and a passage to future greatness. In Australia, he made the cut and then flew back home to Northern Ireland with another €11,500 after finishing 15th on six under and seven shots behind Aaron Baddeley.

Fast forward to Royal Sydney GC on 28th November 2013 and Rory would begin his Australian Open with a -3, 69. This left him seven shots adrift of the Aussie darling Adam Scott who thrilled his fellow Aussies with a sizzling 10 under, 62.

As Scott struggled to show anything like that hot the streak next day, it was Rory who turned on the style. After shooting a super 65, he now shot up the leaderboard to sit only two shots behind the Australian on -10.

It was a role reversal in the third round as Rory only managed a 70, while Scott's 68 gave him a four shot lead going into the last day. It was a lot of ground to make up but in the last group with Scott, he was just one great round away from ending his run of misery.

Actually, the Aussie was just one round away from his own personal milestone. After winning the Australian PGA, he then became the first Australian ever to claim three successive Australian Masters titles when he won it on 23 November.

Now he was bidding to become the sixth man to win the Australian Triple Crown by adding this Australian Open to his resume. Robert Allenby, Peter Lonard, Craig 'Popeye' Parry, Peter Senior and of course Greg 'Shark' Norman had previously achieved the feat.

The duel began and soon it became evident that Rory was keyed up and determined while Scott just looked a little off colour. Maybe the enormity of history allied to Rory's dazzling displays started to unsettle him.

Some great iron play and birdies from Rory had eaten into his lead and he had yet to make anything happen. It was one of those days when nothing would fall for him, but it still looked like Rory had too much to do and Scott would run out the victor.

Even though he was only a single shot under par for the day, Scott stood on the 18th with a one shot lead and a little piece of immortality beckoning. Horror of horrors and how many times have we witnessed it – a few minutes from home and he made a mess of it.

He bogeyed the final hole and when Rory rammed home a 15-foot birdie, he led for the very first time and where it mattered most – at the death. Rory was 2013 Australian Open Champion.

The first prize of A\$225,000 (€155,000) did not matter. The ghosts of previous darkness had been exorcised and all round the green you could almost hear his actual sighs of relief. But in that moment, his sportsmanship shone through.

In an act of real human virtue and character, remarked upon by many observers and again compared to other golfers of much less humility, he expressed a heartfelt sorry for his vanquished opponent. He sympathized with Adam Scott for gate-crashing his big day.

Not before he firstly apologized to large numbers of the 20,000 crowd milling around the presentation party on the 18th afterwards. And of course being in Australia he was quick thinking in knowing that he also had to be politically correct.

He lamented:

It's hard not to feel some sort of guilt the way I won it. Adam is a phenomenal golfer, a great competitor and probably an even better guy. I feel a bit sorry that I was the one that ruined the Triple Crown for him but I'm happy and Adam should be proud of himself. He's a credit to the game and to this country.

As regards his own goals and ambitions, he was obviously thrilled to win again. It was his first title in just over a year and it staved off his slide down the world rankings. After the win he was back up to world number six. His relief was palpable as he beamed:

It's been a frustrating year but I've worked hard and it's been a process trying to get back to winning golf tournaments again. So it's really nice to do that today.

Then, with the long gleaming silver trophy (similar to the Claret Jug) packed away, it was off to catch a flight from Sydney to California for his last unofficial event of the year: the Tiger Woods-promoted World Challenge.

With Christmas just a few weeks away, on the flight he was no doubt dreaming and making plans ahead. He was thinking of specific plans for a very special person who was the first to receive his phone call and his news of victory.

That person was Caroline Wozniacki.

Chapter 11

'WOZZILROY'

The vast majority of people, including the media, do not know for sure the precise point at which the lives of Caroline Wozniacki and Rory McIlroy first crashed headlong into each other.

Only Caroline, Rory, their closest friends and family know for sure; even then, some of those may be a little hazy about precise details. For there are all sorts of differing stories bandied about.

I do not pretend to know either – and it is none of my business. I would prefer to talk about golf. But relationships have had a big impact on Rory's golf career so it is very much part of his story.

What seems pretty sure, to my mind, is that somebody in the upper echelons of the golf or tennis world brought the two together. If that is true then Rafael Nadal, the current men's world number one tennis player, could have been the matchmaker!

A little while after Rory split from his first girlfriend Holly Sweeney, he met up with his good friend Rafa. He was also introduced to Andy Murray at Wimbledon, so he was getting 'introduced' to the inner sanctum of the tennis circuit in a big way.

McIlroy was even invited to take his place seated in the Royal box and, short of having a fist full of popcorn with a beer, or strawberries with cream, he really loved watching the top tennis matches from there.

He was steadily becoming an avid follower of the game and of Nadal in particular. There is little doubt that he was also invited by the Spaniard to watch him practise on some of the outside courts – and perhaps for a short lesson or two in serve and volleying.

Therefore the course plotted for Rory to meet 'Caro' was probably charted by Nadal. Both he and Rory were communicating quite a bit by mobile phone. During one of these exchanges, Rafa apparently passed on Caroline's phone number to Rory, or his to her.

Tabloid sensationalism and salaciousness decreed in one story that Nadal had Caroline Wozniacki's phone number because she liked him. It went on to say that Nadal was only interested in being totally focussed on tennis and besides, he already had a girlfriend.

So the story goes that, knowing Caroline was single, and Rory had recently become single again, he put the two of them in touch. Of all the stories, it does seem as if there is credence in the Nadal involvement somewhere along the line.

Rory and Caroline met shortly after Wimbledon. The two were spotted over at the World Heavyweight title fight in Germany between Vladimir Klitschko and David Haye on 2 July 2011.

Wozniacki, who is an avid fan of worldwide sport and is a Liverpool supporter, tweeted after the bout in Hamburg's Imtech Arena: 'Fantastic fight! Also met Rory McIlory who was sitting just behind me. Really down to earth great guy.'

The fact that Rory sat behind Caroline was probably a ploy. Both were getting to know one another ('getting fixed up' in Irish parlance) and they did not want to feed the tabloids with any stories.

A week after attending the big fight night in London, Caroline celebrated her 21st Birthday. On that day, 11 July, Rory tweeted: 'Happy birthday! You're getting old'

Caroline replied: 'haha I know! But still not as old as you. At least now you will be able to buy me a drink in the US haha..'

Three days later Rory teed off in the British Open held at Royal St. George's in Kent. After enduring a miserable weekend with bad scores in dreadful weather, he stayed on for a little while to congratulate Darren Clarke on winning his first major there.

Sharing in Darren's celebrations whetted his appetite for something else he was eagerly looking forward to that evening. In the previous days, he had arranged his first private date with Caroline. It was most probably the first time they were alone together.

She was doing a photo shoot on Sunday 17 July in London for Adidas and Stella McCartney. So they arranged to meet close to where Rory would be disembarking from the British Rail train he took to Waterloo.

Not far from Waterloo Station, a witness dining in the All Bar One restaurant spotted the pair eating. After they had finished their meal, they were spotted leaving and sharing a kiss goodbye in the street outside.

The excitement of meeting at the big fight night and the rendezvous at a London restaurant was just the very beginning. The couple would arrange a whole series of meetings in more exotic locations all around the world over the next two years.

In between those beautiful breakaways, Rory visited her home in Monaco as well as meeting her parents in Denmark. Later, Caroline would meet Rory's parents and stay with him at his plush new home (complete with mini golf course) in Holywood.

When Rory later sold that property, Caroline would jet into Palm Beach Gardens in Florida where Rory had purchased a beautiful lavish $15 million mansion with a mainly black and white interior theme.

At an American football game in late August, Rory, wearing the No 96 blue jersey of Yale University, presented Caroline with her very own club. He then planted a huge kiss on her lips after being egged on by the entire boisterous team.

The Titleist 'Vokey' 60 degree wedge, which costs around £25, was engraved across the top of the blade with the word 'Wozzilroy', a portmanteau of Wozniacki and McIlroy that a British tabloid came up with.

McIlroy was not only endorsing his liking for the newspaper term, he was also announcing to the world that, at that moment, the two were now a union. Interestingly, Rory and Caroline were following an illustrious line of sporting couples.

Many hailed from the world of tennis, such as Steffi Graf and Andre Agassi; Chris Evert and Greg Norman and, more recently, Kim Clijsters and Lleyton Hewitt; Martina Hingis and Sergio Garcia and Ana Ivanovic and Adam Scott.

Christmas 2011 was spent in Thailand with the couple going to visit a Buddhist Shrine. Both were pictured kneeling down at a temple in the beach resort of Hua Hin bowing their heads and with their hands clasped in prayer.

Caroline was playing in a World Tennis charity event on New Year's Day. She commented on how she also visited a market and was delighted to be given a lesson in how to cook Thai food. Rory, who was made an MBE in the Queens Honours list, said:

It is quite humbling to be included in such a list of worthy recipients. Many people on the list have made huge personal sacrifices and contributed significantly to society during their lives. I feel very fortunate.

Eight months after first meeting, and now very much in love, they could not stand being apart for too lengthy a period. So much so that Rory was literally dashing from golf courses to catch planes, trains and automobiles to be with her.

A case in point was Sunday 4 March 2012, which was the day Rory became world number one by winning the Honda Classic. How did he celebrate that feat? He caught a flight from Miami to New York to meet Caroline. But it was to be no ordinary lovey-dovey meeting.

Caroline was playing in Madison Square Garden in an exhibition with Maria Sharapova. Suddenly, Rory was climbing over the courtside barriers in jeans and t-shirt to play a few shots, much to the amusement of the crowd. Enjoying the moment, he said after:

Caroline turned to the crowd and asked if there were any hot guys who wanted to dance with her! And I'm like, well, I don't want anybody else dancing with you so I put my hand up. Thank God she didn't ask me to dance. I was much happier hitting a tennis shot.

The globetrotting and courting continued unabated. No amount of air miles or jet lag seemed to be a barrier. In mid October Caroline joined Rory at the Turkish Airlines World Golf finals where Rory finished last of the eight competitors.

A few days later and Rory was frantically trying to obtain a Russian visa so he could accompany her to Moscow for the Kremlin Cup the following week. Concerning his form in the Turkish event he said:

I'm not that disappointed as I have the afternoon off around the pool. I just came here because I've never played in Turkey and there were some good players here.

They spent a second successive Christmas together – this time in Australia – but not before Caroline had to deny engagement rumours in November (the result of a prank by Serena Williams' boyfriend) and Rory had to deny similar rumours just before Christmas.

Wozniacki was sensationally knocked out in the first round of the Brisbane International by a qualifier. But for the next week, photos circumnavigated the world of her and Rory having so much fun Down Under.

There was a trip to the Sydney Opera House and the undoubted highlight was the Sydney Tower Skywalk. Dressed in blue boiler suits high above the skyscrapers of Sydney, and well protected with straps, they walked along the edge of the top of the tower.

With beaming smiling faces behind dark sunglasses, they both took selfies to post on twitter. There was also a 'sky photo' of them on top of New York's Empire State Building (I hope you bought her one of the many varieties of 'King Kong' dolls Rors!).

At the end of that first week in January it was back to the grindstone for both. Rory had to play in Abu Dhabi the following week but as we have already seen, this was to be a year when he found it the toughest going of his golfing life.

In contrast to 2012, he fell into the doldrums in 2013. Apart from the rumors of marriage, he also had to make do with disquiet among his fellow professional and golf pundits who were not best happy with all the time he was talking away from golf.

Then at the Honda Classic in March – where exactly one year before he became world number one by winning it and then jetting straight to New York to see Caroline – he walked off the course and out of the tournament. He also had a go at the media over his love life:

I've read what's been written and just because I had a bad day on the golf course [walked off] and Caroline lost in Malaysia, it doesn't mean we're breaking up. Its sport and I'd like to keep my private life as private as possible. Everything on that front is great

and I'm looking forward to seeing her next week when she jets into Miami.

The media smelt blood and they went straight for the jugular vein. They felt their relationship was on the rocks and they would stop at nothing to print it. They were completely wrong.

I still cannot believe how completely wrong the British and Irish media got it. So much so that I contacted many people I knew in the industry to tell them so. Reporters, writers, editors, broadcasters – I told them all but they just shrugged their shoulders.

It was as if they did not care if they were wrong. The saying goes that 'there is no such thing as bad publicity', as it sells. So they just built up and sensationalized their version of the story for the public.

What makes the whole episode even more astonishing to me is that they were (and are) playing a very dangerous game. It seems as if the painful lessons learnt from past huge libel cases do not register.

The media seemed to be taking a gamble that Rory and Caroline were too young and too busy to be bothered taking them through the courts. They are playing Russian roulette. From the last book, here is what one tabloid 'columnist' wrote about Rory splitting with Holly.

Like all these young men who think grass is always greener on the other fairway, Rory will learn the hard way that the burger never tastes as good as the steak. Here's to Holly – a classy birdie even when Rory's pursuing a bit of rough.

It is such a dangerous game they play. Newspaper bosses take note of this – at some stage in the future, some couple will produce a dossier of proof of being at weddings, parties, christenings, hotels or wherever to counteract all the days, weeks and months of untruths.

An Irish Sports editor said to me: 'On what basis do you believe they have not broken up?' and a young woman with a website told me 'Nope, they've split end of story'.

Here is that basis of what I believed back then. It was a firm belief based on painstakingly doing what the Irish and British media did not do: research, as well as going to sources in Denmark.

Firstly, at the Honda Classic Rory denied it. He also said things were 'great' and that Caroline was 'jetting into Miami''. Secondly – and most important of all – no family member or friend from either side came forward to ever say they were breaking up.

On that last note, Caroline replied to what Rory said at the Honda when stating: 'I'm so tired of the rumours. They occur when Rory and I are apart a few days or when we do not talk on twitter. All is well and there is not much more to say about it.'

Yet the media for weeks and weeks went on – until they fell silent because they had nothing more to go on. The really unbelievable thing about the whole episode was that across the North Sea in Denmark, no media outlets were saying any such thing.

The reason for that was simple – there was nothing to report. No concrete facts and that is why the Danes do things properly. They act within the cardinal rules of proper journalism as Rene Schroder, news director of Extra Bladet explained to me on 16 October:

We have a policy whereby when we write a story about a couple splitting up, at least one of them has to confirm it to us. Or any other evidence like 'Rory caught on camera with another girl'.

It is no more than two days since Caroline denied any split to us. Enclosed for you is the link (in Danish) where she denies everything to our tennis reporter.

So there you have it in a nutshell. It was a similar story from Lars Andersson of Tekstwerk when I got in touch with him. So why did the Irish and British media report a split over a long period of time? There was no split – Rory and Caroline told us!

Furthermore, a month before this in September, the media ran stories that Rory was out dining and dating Irish model Nadia Forde in Dublin after his afternoon meeting with former US President Bill Clinton. But she was quoted as saying: 'Rory is in a relationship and I'm single – very single.'

I may be wrong but this is what I actually believe went on between McIlroy and Wozniacki. Caroline was doing poorly in events while Rory hit a woeful patch from very early in 2013 and was under severe pressure using Nike clubs.

Perhaps the two met and agreed that they had to cool things down and stop all their jet-setting for the sakes of their careers, which were suffering. They probably agreed to meet on special occasions or when Caroline would be playing nearby in the States.

So even though the couple agreed on this, when they cooled their tweets and meetings the media smelt blood. When the media went into overdrive, and the attention became unbearable, Rory and Caroline were panicked into showing that they were still an item.

They eventually resumed tweeting and, in time, they would meet up again at various events. And the biggest proof that they were still very much together came when Caroline won the Luxembourg Open.

Just five days after my pleas to so many media people here – and to my sources in Denmark who stated correctly that there was no split – Rory McIlroy sent his girlfriend a very loving message of congratulations for the entire world to see.

On 21 October, the day after Caroline won her first ranking event for a year, he tweeted: '#21 #luxembourg #mygirl @CaroWozniacki.' – 21 is the number of titles she had won. 'My Girl' finally forced the media into total and absolute submission. A stunned silence.

Just over two months later, Caroline and Rory spent their third successive Christmas together. It was going to be one of the happiest festive seasons of their lives and not just because Caroline won a title in October and Rory won the Australian Open in November.

Those wins put the smiles firmly back on their faces to seal a nice satisfactory end to respective poor seasons. But it was nothing to the smiles that lit up their faces and the whole of Sydney on New Years Eve when he proposed to her. Let Rory tell the story:

I was sweating a lot. I'd an idea she'd say 'yes' but you never really know until it actually happens. We were out on a boat in Sydney Harbour for New Years Eve, just in front of the Opera House, and the fireworks were going off. I guess there was a little bit of romance involved, and yeah, she was surprised.

I had an idea it was something she wanted and hoped she'd say 'yes' and she did. I'd been thinking about it for a while and I asked her parents in December. If you get engaged you plan on spending the rest of your life with that person, so it's a big decision. But I feel like she's definitely the right girl for me.

****

The thing is that this was a crucial building block in the redevelopment and reconstruction of Rory Phase two which brought him two majors, a big event at Wentworth and a WGC event.

These wins, by his own admission, were where he 'played the greatest golf of my life.' There will be a Rory Phase three and Phase four because the bottom line is that Rory's form will dip again in the future.

When it does he will have to change something and sometimes that means a huge sacrifice. I believe that one such sacrifice will be the parting of the ways with his caddy J P Fitzgerald.

The thing is, this should bear no slight on J P. He is actually a top class, first rate, A1 Caddy.

Chapter 12

THE SPLIT

Date: 21 May 2014
Time: Early morning
Location: Dublin City, Ireland
Means: Electronic message (Email/Fax)
Subject: Rory McIlroy Statement

There is no right way to end a relationship that has been so important to two people.

The problem is mine. The wedding invites issued at the weekend made me realise that I wasn't ready for all that marriage entails.

I wish Caroline all the happiness she deserves and thank her for the great times we have had. I will not be saying anymore about our relationship in any setting.

Date: 21 May 2014
Time: Afternoon
Location: Wentworth Golf Club, Virginia Water, Surrey, South of England
Means: Pre BMW Championship Press Conference
Subject: Rory McIlroy takes questions on shock news

Michael Gibbons: Well, Rory, many thanks for joining us. I'm sure everyone here appreciates you coming in today. We've all seen your statement this morning so I'm just going to hand it over to you to start us off.

Rory: Yeah, obviously quite a difficult time for Caroline and myself, and I think the statement really said it all this morning. It was mutual and amicable and we both thought it was the best for us, the best for both of us. Time to move on and I think I've said all that I need to say. Just want to get my head into golf this week and concentrate on the tournament and try and do well. Been playing well. The form's been good. Just want to dive straight into it and keep myself somewhat busy and just try and have a good week on the course.

MG: Thank you. We'll take some questions.

Q. Realistically, how possible is that going to be to be able to concentrate on your golf?

R: I'm not going to lie. It's going to be very difficult. But you know, at least when I get inside the ropes, just try and concentrate on the shot at hand. But yeah, it's obviously going to be difficult.

Q. Were you tempted to pull out at any stage because of this, because it can't be easy with so much turmoil going on even though you've perhaps become almost used to it over the last 18 months, haven't you?

R: No, I didn't think there was any reason to do that. There's no good time to sort of end a relationship I guess. No, I just – I made a commitment to be here. It's your European Tour's flagship event. I'm very proud to be part of the European Tour. The European Tour have been very good to me over the last number of years, and I thought it was my duty to come back and play in this event. You know, once I gave my word that I would, I wasn't going to go back on it.

Q. Will this have any effect on your schedule in the next month or so? Might you play more events now?

R: I haven't – I don't know. My schedule right now is here, Memorial and U.S. Open, Irish Open, Scottish Open, British Open. I don't think that's going to change.

Q. **You had that sort of double-delight in Sydney last year, winning the Australian Open and also being on Sydney Harbour when you proposed to Caroline. How tough a decision was it for you?**

R: Look, I think I'm no different than anyone else. Everyone has been through break ups and it's obviously very, very difficult. But look, I'm here to try and concentrate on this week and answer questions about golf and that's what I'm going to do.

Q. **At least you're at a golf course that you love [laughter follows].**

R: [Laughs back].

Q. **Can you just talk about your history at Wentworth?**

R: Yeah, look, I've enjoyed my times here. I think it's a beautiful golf course. I've got great memories of the place from coming back and watching the World Match Play in the early 2000s as a kid. I've struggled on the course personally since they made the changes. I'm trying to go in this week with the mind-set of not getting frustrated and not – just trying to play to my spots and not be frustrated that I might only get to hit driver two or three times a round and feel like my advantage of my length is taken away from me. I'm just going to try – you know – just accept that you've got to plot your way around this golf course and not be overly aggressive. And that's really what I have to try and do – just sort of reign it in a little bit. But it's a great event. It's always well supported by all the Europeans that come back and play on the PGA Tour. It's the European Tour's flagship event. BMW are a great supporter of golf around the world, and this tournament deserves the best players and the best field, and it gets that. You know, hopefully I can put in a performance that's a little better than it has been the last few years.

Q. **I think you were saying on the previous Sunday, the same kind of thing about Sawgrass, learning how to play the course. Same thing applies here?**

R: Yeah, exact same thing. I think it's a very similar, the style of golf that you need to play here is very similar to the style of golf you need to play around Sawgrass. Again you don't get to hit many drivers at Sawgrass. You have to be not cautious, but just you have to position your ball in the right spots and just be patient. I feel like I'm getting better at that. I had my best finish at Sawgrass a couple weeks ago, a couple of top 10s in a row there, which is a big improvement. As I said, hopefully this week I can do something similar.

Q. **How much have you looked forward to today's Pro-Am pairing?**

R: Yeah, it's going to be nice. I've been a Manchester United fan my whole life, and getting to play with three Manchester United legends [Phil Neville, Peter Schmeichel and Teddy Sheringham] is going to be a nice afternoon. I remember watching the Champions League final in '99 when United beat Munich in Barcelona, and it was a very memorable night. Obviously all those three guys were involved, and yeah, it's going to be a nice afternoon.

MG: Rory, I'm sure everyone joins me in wishing you well, thanks.

Date: 22 May 2014
Time: Mid morning
Location: Monte Carlo, Monaco
Means: Twitter Message (Tweet)
Subject: Caroline Wozniacki's first response

It's a hard time for me right now. Thanks for all the sweet

messages! Happy I support Liverpool right now because I know
I'll never walk alone.

Shock! That is the very first thing to say about the sudden split.
Even though the media had speculated wrongly on a breaking up the
previous year, this took the world completely by surprise because of
the beautiful New Years Eve engagement in Australia.

I certainly felt sad and I still do. I do not know why as I'm no
soppy romantic. Perhaps it was because they were such good friends
who wore their hearts on their sleeves. Despite mega money and
wealth, they really loved being free and ordinary like the rest of us.
That probably reflected similar sentiments to others who were
actually at the press conference. The Irish Independent's greatly
respected and hugely experienced golf writer Karl MacGinty
captured the mood brilliantly:

This was an incredibly courageous effort by the 25-year-old whose
sombre demeanour, heavy eyes and solemn words left absolutely
no room for doubt about his heartache.

As Rory left the interview, an American lady from the New York
Times added her sentiments saying:

How impressive was that. Everyone knows how hard it is to break
up and there were moments when I wanted to go up there and give
him a hug.

Rory was genuinely gutted. There is no doubt about that and the
following day the Irish Mirror's front page captured Rory's facial
expression of biting his chin under a headline:

'RORY'S AGONY'

So 'Wozzilroy' was engraved by Rory on one of his irons to
consummate his relationship with Wozniacki. But alas, there would
be no engraving of anything on any wedding bands. It was over.

Caroline Wozniacki was really upset. She later revealed that Rory just called her, a short 10 minute phone call, to end it. She felt hurt and betrayed that their great friendship whittled down to that.

But she should know that Rory cried buckets of tears too. Maybe he even cried over a much longer period than she realises. It tore the heart out of him to do that. If you want proof of it, just look at his emotional press conference before the PGA at Wentworth.

McIlroy does not feign or put on emotions. What we have all grown to love about this genius is the fact that he wears his heart on his sleeve. He had 'to be cruel to be kind' for both their sakes.

He could not arrange to meet Caroline to end it because it would have been too emotional and galling that they would probably not be able to end it together. It was a cruel way to end it from afar but ultimately, this really was for the best for both of them.

Over the course of the following months they would reap enormous benefits from their new found freedom. They entertained the world for two years and let us be honest – we all loved watching the pair popping up in photos in the most exotic places and in sport.

Did we not marvel at Caroline in a white caddy suit carrying the bag for Rors at our proud Irish Open? Did we not love that moment where she asked Rory to come on court in America and have a few tennis shots with her – or the putt she sank at Augusta?

They were a breath of fresh air and a beautiful young couple. Top level professional sport and business can be cruel. However, when their careers finish, the love that was suppressed for the good of their careers will rekindle and flow again in a different sense.

Over many years into the future, many memories will flood back into their separate lives. Their lovely honest hearts will flutter at the thoughts and feelings behind those images until the day they die.

In the short term, their love will remain strong in an altogether new setting. They will feel a deep fondness, gratitude and pride for inspiring each other to greatness that would follow for both.

After the shock had sunk in with an obviously distraught Caroline, and the cold sobering thoughts that this was very real, she had to do certain things in the coming days and weeks which must have torn at her heart.

The invitations to a lavish wedding at New York's Rockefeller Centre which she was preparing to send out, together with the

£100,000 gold engagement ring Rory put on her finger, were put away in some obscure place where the sun never shines.

And then there was one final act. All her photos of Rory, in her homes and on her Twitter and Facebook pages, along with tweets and messages and cuddly toys and travel mementoes, had to be taken down.

Of course the speculation then went into overdrive on the part of the media. There were all sorts of reasons put forward as to 'why'. Some bordered on the ridiculous while some were quite plausible and possible.

Perhaps the silliest reason put forward for their parting, in my view, was the photo Caroline posted of Rory beside her on a beach resort. It was a less than complimentary photo of him, while she and good friend Serena Williams had a right laugh over it.

Apparently Rory was not best pleased. To me, it is rubbish to suggest that many months later Rory would be holding that against her to the point of ending their engagement. One thing seems certain – the real reason will be revealed in a future autobiography.

My own personal view is that any one, or all, of three things contributed to their parting. All three are based on actual facts that affect relationships – be it current or past loves or people we know – and which seemed to afflict Rory and Caroline too:

(i) The most important reason was the one which also caused Rory to split on no less than three previous occasions. Call it 'Betterment of Career' and you have Rory leaving Holly Sweeney, IMG and Horizon.

(ii) The second reason is 'Arguments'. It is well known that everybody has disagreements. The saying goes 'you wouldn't be a couple if you didn't argue'. As sure as they had their first date and first kiss, Rory and Caroline also had their first argument (arguments can be silent moods as well).

(iii) Lastly, but by no means least, is 'No Future'. There is a very true saying: 'long distance relationships don't work'.

For the first reasoning, Rory's career was in the doldrums. Despite halting his slide with that win in Australia, he did not win a major in 2013. With Nike on board, success is measured in terms of majors and rankings so he simply had to be successful – and soon.

In order to get back to winning majors again, Rory had to make massive changes in his life. He had to cut out all the extra baggage of weekends away in exotic locations and that could only mean one thing.

The second reason is that of disagreements between the pair. If you look again at their initial statements on the split, you will see that there is only one common denominator in both – they express love for their respective favourite football teams.

Why, on such an important matter, did Caroline feel the need to put in her love for Liverpool? It was also noticeable how Rory perked up and came alive when he was asked about playing the pro-am with three Manchester United legends.

There seems little doubt both had differences of opinion on matters between their football teams. Manchester United endured a desperate season while Liverpool almost won the Premiership.

To make matters worse, Liverpool did the double over United. At the start of the season they won 1-0 at Anfield and towards the end of the season at Old Trafford, Liverpool humiliated them 3-0.

In a season of woe for Manchester United, Caroline probably had one two many 'digs' at Rory and on Twitter. She also seems to have a soft spot for present and former Liverpool players, including fellow Dane, Daniel Agger, as well as Slovakian, Martin Skrtel.

Do not for one moment downplay this. Sport, like politics and religion, can become a very emotive subject amongst people. Furthermore, both football clubs have a history of not seeing eye-to-eye. This transmits to a great majority of their supporters.

On another matter – was there a disagreement regarding wedding guests? Was there a golfer or soccer player who was not flavour of the month with one of them to the point where a serious objection and 'silence argument' took place?

Another source of tension could have been time. Rory was jetting all over the world to spend quality time with Caroline. Perhaps occasionally, when he arrived and could not wait to see her, he felt she was not fully giving of her time to him or vice versa.

These are things that happen to all of us and arguments, particularly in the early stages of relationships, are one of the biggest causes of splits. So Rory was also right in what he said, that: 'I'm no different than anyone else – everyone has been through break-ups'.

The third point really speaks for itself: they really had no future. It is a well known fact long distance relationships rarely (if ever) work. As well as that, they were far too young to settle down in their early 20s.

With that in mind, there was one subject not brought up by the media – *pre-nuptial agreements/alimony.* Rory could have had the serious implications of this pointed out to him by his elder advisors.

Tiger Woods' divorce could have served as a sobering reminder to him of future pitfalls surrounding a possible marriage split of his own. In 2010, Fox News reported that Woods settled on a $750 million alimony figure with Elin Nordegren!

It was the biggest American divorce settlement in history with Elin also getting custody of the children. Most of the colossal sum was a sort of insurance policy whereby she agreed to remain silent on his alleged affairs with three named women and up to 17 others.

So most certainly, there were huge risks for Rory rushing into marriage at the age of 25.

A future of unlimited potential to be gained from their respective sporting careers meant that, in truth, they were just a little too young to settle down. It was for the best, sentiments echoed entirely by Europe's 2012 Ryder Cup Captain Jose Maria Olazabal.

When he was asked for his views on the split he lamented:

It is tough for golfers to have relationships. We spend a lot of time away from home and it is hard to keep a relationship going. There are some good things about golf but also some not so good things. I wish Caroline and Rory all the best. Their time will come. They are very young.

Chapter 13

HOYLAKE AHOY!

Sensationally, Rory McIlroy went on to win that BMW Championship in England. The very tournament he held a shaky record in, and where it seemed more important to turn up because all the top Europeans were travelling to play in it.

Just three days after pouring his heart out to the world over his decision to part with Caroline Wozniacki, he won. It was a mysterious win. You could never say that Rory set the world alight with his golf that week.

For the first few days, and somewhat understandably, he seemed to be just going through the motions. A first round 68 was promising but a 71 the next day followed by a 69 indicated that a win was never really on the cards as he trailed leader Tomas Bjorn by seven shots.

It was as if his thoughts were off course – wondering if he had made the right decision; looking and feeling the crowds response to it and gauging how the players and the golf world had taken the news.

Caroline's fellow Dane, Tomas Bjorn, was one of those to commiserate with Rory and this probably helped to lift a weight off his shoulders. The crowd warmed to him as well and all of a sudden he began to feel free and ready to express himself on the course.

The chains and shackles had been removed. So far behind going into the final round, he could loosen his elbow with nothing to lose. He shot a magnificent 66 as Bjorn, who held a five shot lead over Donald, really threw the tournament away with a disastrous +3, 75.

Beaming with delight as he held the trophy and a cheque for just short of €800,000, Rory admitted as much as he said:

I'm not exactly sure what I am feeling right now. It has obviously been a week of very mixed emotions. I'm sitting here looking at this trophy going: 'How the hell did it happen this week?' But it did. I feel happy that I have won obviously but it has been a weird week.

However, the win finally rewarded him after he had been ultra consistent in the majority of tournaments played since the start of the 2014 season. He hit the ground running in Abu Dhabi back in January when he was runner-up.

A fortnight later at the Dubai Desert Classic he opened up with a superb -9, 63. This helped him to a top 10 finish before he jetted home to Florida where he was about to take the US Tour by storm over the next three months.

He may have walked out of the Honda Classic the previous year but 12 months on, he thrilled the locals by opening with yet another 63. Further rounds of 66 and 69 put him in position for a sensational win but a 74 spoiled what would have been a perfect return.

Nevertheless a cool half million dollars and runner-up finish showed that he was in great form with one eye on the US Masters a month later. Before Augusta he finished 25th in the Cadillac and a week before the first major finished seventh in the Houston Open.

You just had to admire where he and his coach had come from. No missed cuts to mid-April, two 63s and two runners-up positions was a total contrast and the perfect tonic and antidote to the miserable year before. But the one that really mattered was up next.

Rory stated previously that, since his 'Masters meltdown', he always seems to throw in a bad nine holes at Augusta. It happened again when he shot a +5, 77 in the second round which after a modest opening 71 put him in grave danger of missing the cut.

He just about made it with another 71 but those rounds were never going to trouble Bubba Watson who went on to win it by three shots. A final effort of 69 brought Rory up to a share of eighth with the likes of veteran Bernhard Langer.

It was another top 10 but the Masters is now becoming one big psychological worry for him. Forever at the back of his mind will be the thought that he may never get a better chance of winning than in

2011 when he led the field by four shots on the final day.

Augusta is a very mysterious course. It is governed by great golfing gods looking at you from every direction. The spirits of great souls past pervade that glorious piece of golfing heaven.

Winds seem to blow in and across from different directions; they can cause confusion and the haunting sounds of birds which echo through the valleys and shady areas are enough to put you off your concentration.

Irish legend and 'World Golf Hall of Fame' recipient Christy O'Connor Senior never wished to play the Masters and never did despite numerous invites. He was not the only one.

Lee Trevino could not abide it and only played on sufferance as the PGA threatened to throw the book at him. When he did eventually come back and play it, he preferred to stay in his room and mend his clubs rather than socialise with those who forced his hand.

Phil Mickelson was exasperated for years in trying to win the event. Butch Harmon told him that he would not win unless he modified his aggressive driving. Although Phil persisted and eventually climbed into a Green Jacket, there is a lesson for Rory.

What he must do to win a Masters is to start playing 'smart golf' around there. He has laughed about 'the cabins' incident and gone back to inspect it but what he has probably not thought about is the fatalistic message behind that pivotal moment.

Many sportsmen and women have their superstitions. Equally their sports are full of them, and as a studious observer of sport since I was a young boy, it is actually remarkable how time and again many of them ring true.

Football has its 'if you don't convert your chances you'll be punished' and 'luck evens itself out', while in snooker they say 'the balls won't forgive you'. There are powerful forces at work everywhere.

Why did Rory clip that tree? He could not believe what happened. It is the same as asking Tiger Woods why he suddenly decided to start leaving his driver in his bag. Tiger knew he had to begin playing smart golf instead of power golf. It won him majors.

At Augusta, Rory: strategically and with great care plot your way, whereby you must start to caress and use finesse. Love that ball and love the course. Marvel at it bouncing into the nice carpeted fairways and greens; look around to feel and understand its history.

Only then you will begin to understand how you must give yourself as a sacrifice to their gods. Once they know they have your love and respect, you will be rewarded. Power, aggression and the wrong frame of mind are frowned upon.

Those forces governing the course at Wells Fargo adore Rory and the feeling is mutual. Even the sound of that tournament is phonetically one of the nicest in golf – the Wells Fargo at Quail Hollow.

It must make Rory want to eat quail for dinner and quail eggs for breakfast because he is rarely out of the top 10 there and holds the course record. So it proved again at Wells Fargo as three weeks later he matched his Masters finish with another eighth place.

He went from one extreme to the other the following week when he once again tried to climb and conquer his own personal Everest at the Players in Sawgrass. It did not look too good after he opened with rounds of 70 and 74 to just about make the weekend.

Martin Kaymer opened with a -9, 63 and was never caught. Rory did improve with a 69 in the third round and he closed with a fine 66 which helped him soar up the leaderboard to a share of sixth place.

Those last two rounds will give him confidence confronting Sawgrass in future. The previous year he had opened with a 66 and finished tied eighth and this time he closed with the same score to again finish in the top 10, so he looks like reaching the summit soon.

At the Memorial Tournament three weeks later he registered another good result when finishing just outside the top 10 in 15th. He was still showing brilliant consistency but without ever threatening to take an event by the scruff of the neck and win handsomely.

A fortnight after Ohio came the second major of the year, the 114th US Open. Rory was coming into Pinehurst, North Carolina, in great confidence on the back of excellent consistency.

His game was in good shape and he was hoping for just one final push to land the win his form merited and his third major. But Martin Kaymer, who blew the field away after his first round in the 'Fifth Major', blitzed the entire US Open field at the halfway point.

US Opens are noted for being such tough assignments that

normally someone under par or level par can win the event. Such was the case the previous year when Justin Rose won his first major in the US Open at Merion, Pennsylvania on one over par with Mickelson second on three over.

That was nothing compared to 2006 when Geoff Ogilvy triumphed at Winged Foot recording a four round total of six over. In 2007 at Oakmont, Angel Cabrera went one better by winning on five over!

After two rounds, the German broke several records by carding 65, 65 for 10 under. It must be stressed that it was even better than Rory's 11 under in 2011 because this was a par-70 course to Rory's par 72 at Congressional (Rory was -13 through 35 holes). With Kaymer on fire, Rory was never really in with a chance after his opening salvo of 71 and 68. He was nine shots behind and, like the rest of the field in these brutal tests, he regressed after that.

Further rounds of 74 and 73 meant he finished on six over which was still good enough for 23rd. Only three men finished under par. Kaymer matched Rory's eight shot winning margin in 2011 by winning on nine under from Erik Compton and Rickie Fowler on one under. Fourth was one over par.

The thing about this result which depressed McIlroy was that only two majors remained and he was now in great danger of successive seasons without major success. All of his consistency bore no fruit.

More to the point, and if you ignore his last gasp Australian triumph, then he was almost one and a half years without a win in Europe or the US. Make no bones about it – Nike would have been concerned. He said:

I'm wondering how he [Kaymer] did it, yeah. It's tough. I think I've made a total of nine birdies this week. I don't see anymore out there. It's tough. Obviously, if you limit the mistakes, you might end up a couple under par for the week, because you're always going to make a few mistakes. But to do what he did – I think it's nearly more impressive than what I did at Congressional.

Rory had only four days until he teed up in the Irish Open at Fota Island Resort in Cork. To make matters even worse, when he arrived at the Southern Ireland course, his Nike clubs were nowhere in sight.

United Airlines had somehow managed to lose them in transit and a frantic search was underway to locate them. They were eventually found but it did not do much for his preparations and he ended up missing the cut.

The clubs issue contributed to his first round 74 but he fought like a tiger the next day to make the cut. He failed by the narrowest of margins after a 69 and was clearly frustrated, gutted and embarrassed afterwards as he explained:

It's very frustrating. To make six birdies an eagle and shoot just two under means there were a lot of mistakes and wasteful shots. To miss the cut here for the second year in a row is not a nice position to be in. It is very disappointing.

****

On 18 June, totally unexpected and out of the blue, Rory announced at the Irish Open in Fota Island to a ripple of applause that he would represent Ireland in the Olympics. It was a huge relief and load off his mind as no doubt it was for many in Ireland. He said:

It's just a continuation of what I've always done really. I represented Ireland at Boys and Youths level in European and World Championships and just because I'm now a professional playing for money, it doesn't change that.

When he was asked if it had been a big decision and if he was relieved, he revealed:

Not really because when I had a little time to myself and I sat down and really thought about it, as I said it was just a continuation of what I've always done. So I'll be delighted and I'm really looking forward to pulling on the Irish jersey in Brazil in 2016.

In the circumstances, it was galling for McIlroy to miss the cut at the Irish Open. In fact it was to be his only M/C of the entire season on the US and European tour. He has stated he badly wants to win his home Open. There are several reasons for that:

He is Irish and was helped and nurtured by the GUI; Padraig Harrington and Shane Lowry have won it in recent years; he wants to become only the fifth Irishman to win it in almost 40 years since Christy O'Connor Junior won the inaugural event in 1975.

So it would be a major blot on his resume if he fails. That is not to mention the great list of illustrious names to have won it – Ben Crenshaw, Hubert Green, Sam Torrance, Seve, Bernhard Langer, Ian Woosnam, Ollie, Sir Nick Faldo, Monty and Sergio Garcia.

Many people felt that Rory wanted to 'buy an Irish Open' with the announcement a week before the 2014 Ryder Cup that his company would sponsor the 2015 Irish Open as it moved to Royal County Down.

Of course this is total nonsense as he has to physically go out and win it. It is also nice for the 'Rory Foundation Irish Open' to be held in beautiful County Down where Rory knows the course so well.

I do however feel strongly our Irish Open should also be reinstated at two other courses where I believe Rory would have a great chance of winning.

Portmarnock last staged it in 2003 and it would be so romantic for Rory to win there where all the legends have won.

Baltray in County Louth is a beautiful links course which would suit his game enormously. It is compact and fair and I was privileged to see a young Henrik Stenson play it in 2004 along with Luke Donald and Woosie. Tellingly, Shane Lowry won there in 2009.

Rory took three weeks off until he returned a week before the British Open at Royal Aberdeen for the Scottish Open. A superb opening round of -7, 64 was so good that it was put up in flashing lights – *COURSE RECORD!*

It was not to last long as a couple of local Scots became Rory's party poopers.

Scott Jamieson equaled it with 64 in the last round before Stephen Gallacher took possession of the new outright record with a 63 later that afternoon.

Rory's second round told a far different story and a nasty horror habit was forming. He gave the seven shots back shooting 78. His chance of winning was over at the halfway point yet again as he eventually finished nine shots behind Justin Rose despite last rounds of 68 and 67.

Golf Channel's morning edition talked of Rory having an almost 'Freaky Friday' complex where he could not string two great opening rounds together. He was following an opening sub-70 terrific Thursday with a frightful Friday round.

The evidence was there in the preceding weeks with great opening rounds followed by Friday scores of 77 at Augusta, 76 at Wells Fargo, 74 at the Players and a pair of terrible twin 78s at the Memorial and Aberdeen. But Rory left Aberdeen very happy stating: 'I see enough good signs in my game to give me some confidence going into next week.'

Rory had been heavily criticised since the 2011 British Open when he moaned, groaned and complained about the wet and windy conditions. Many golfers expressed their opinions openly for and against Rory.

Men like Tom Watson, Ian Woosnam, Des Smyth and Eamon Darcy felt sympathy for him. In my 2011 book, I sought out the opinions of someone who actually played against him in the heat of amateur competition in wet and windy West of Ireland.

When Rory was 16, he played in the final of the Irish Close Championship at Westport, County Mayo, where he faced Eddie McCormack, a sales representative for a wine company. At 32, Eddie was twice his age.

He recollects that he went 1-up after five holes but on the back nine, Rory began to pull away when he went 4-up. Eddie pulled one back but attributes that to Rory losing a contact lens and he eventually lost 3 and 2.

The Galway man had consistently maintained, even before many in the higher echelons had pointed it out, that Rory would struggle to win a British Open unless he changed one particular facet of his game, as he explained:

Far be it for me to give Rory advice as he is obviously doing so much right over the last few years. But if I was to pinpoint one criticism of his game, I would say that he hits the ball far too high.

It is all very well doing that on a lot of golf courses – particularly inland. But I do feel that is the reason why he has struggled in the British Open. Because of that, he will find it very hard to string four good rounds together in the Open.

In the British Open, as well as in other events like the Irish Open, if he continues to hit the ball so high, it will mean that the ball will be carried by the wind and blown off course from its intended target. So in that aspect of his play, I think he'll have to learn to adapt to the conditions. If he can fade it, or hit the ball lower, which I'm sure is no problem to him, then he can definitely win an Open.

At Hoylake in Liverpool on 17 July, Rory could not have asked for better conditions. There was little or no wind as he went out and shot six under 66. He was extremely pleased with his morning's work, saying:

Anytime you shoot 66 in a British Open you're going to be pleased. We had perfect scoring conditions out there this morning. There was not much wind early on. The wind picked up a bit on the back nine but, yeah, there was plenty of opportunities to make birdies. I was able to take a few of them. Another great start and I'm really looking forward to getting back out there tomorrow. Really I just have to take it one hole at a time, one shot at a time. I know everyone says it and you've heard it a million times, but it's true. That's what I'll be trying to do tomorrow.

Next day Rory started with a bogey on the first hole. It would turn out to be his only dropped shot in 36 holes. He went on to shoot another superb 66 and was now four shots ahead of Dustin Johnson who shot 65.

Not even an intruder on the eighth hole could stop him. To much amusement, a pheasant strolled across his path as he lined up a birdie putt. He and J P shooed it away and then he calmly birdied. Later he chuckled:

I haven't run into that before on a golf course. I might have had a swan or a duck or geese but never a pheasant. It was nice. It didn't put me off.

In the third round, he was unrelenting. His progress continued. A 68 put him on an amazing -16 under after three rounds and he looked home and hosed. He was six shots ahead going into the final day. One statement he made said it all:

I feel like I just have an inner peace on the golf course. I'm very comfortable in this position. I'm very comfortable doing what I'm doing right now. It's hard to describe. I wish I could get into it more often.

He was really telling the world he was in the zone and he was not going to be caught. All his near misses and frustrations were going to be rewarded with one of the biggest prizes in golf. He was fulfilling his boyhood dream as he spoke those words. He was living it.

Only two things could stop him. Another meltdown similar to Augusta 2011 or the forecast bad weather arriving. As we have seen before in these pages with such as Tomas Bjorn and Adam Scott, final rounds can be full of drama. This would be no exception.

It turned out to be one of the greatest Open's since the 1970s when Nicklaus battled it out with Tom Watson and Gary Player. On Sunday 20 July at Hoylake, two gunslingers confronted Rory at the top in a nail-biting shootout – Sergio Garcia and Rickie Fowler.

Rory looked very nervous on the first tee. He was within reach of a huge personal goal. A British Open was nigh and the fulfillment of a boyhood dream. But he was also wary that after some great rounds, the law of averages meant an ordinary or bad round was due.

He could also hear roars signaling players making moves ahead. It seemed game, set and match when Rory sank a lovely birdie on the first green to go -17 under. But the Fat Lady never sings too early in the day. She makes you work to deserve it. Nothing comes easy.

Unbelievably, he made careless bogeys at the par-five fifth and the par-three sixth to slip back to 15 under and when Sergio Garcia eagled the 10th, Rory's lead was down to just two shots. From five shots to two shots in the blink of an eye and Rory's heart was in his mouth.

He steadied his ship on the seventh and eighth holes and it was business as normal after he made consecutive birdies on the ninth and 10th. But just when the wind was taken out of Garcia's sails, so along surfed the American beach boy Rickie Fowler.

You just had to put the kettle on again and admire the wonder of this best of British Opens for decades. There was no let up. Garcia was a determined man that day with fire in his belly while Fowler drove into the zone with fiery headlights in his eyes.

Fowler's birdie blitz was as spectacular as it was unbelievable. He had the Midas touch and when another one went down into the bowl like so many peas, he had also moved to within two shots of the lead after McIlroy birdied the 16th to erase the bogey on the par-three 13th.

That 16th hole drew a sigh of relief from Rory. With a two shot lead on the 17th tee, at that moment you could see him flick the switch from 'attack' mode into 'defensive' mode. Quite literally you could see him relax and detensify (a new word for Oxford) himself.

Not for him were there going to be any heroics or bravado or gung-ho acts. Mickelson blew a US Open doing precisely that but Rory had worked so hard for this. It was time to cruise home by playing the percentages – nothing fancy, just pars.

A par at the dangerous 17th and a Sunday stroll of a par at the par- five final hole was his victory lap. *'Rory McIlroy, 2014 British Open Champion'* was now official and soon he would be hailed as such by the presentation committee.

It was easy at the start, it was easy at the end, but in the middle he was frantically splashing about in the deep end. Ultimately though, it ended in a controlled performance of some majesty.

Rosy, his mother, ran on to the green for a monster hug while dad Gerry was probably trying to collect his winnings from the bookies. Ten years before he and three friends placed £100 at 500/1 on Rory winning the Open by the age of 25. Nice one! Go collect, Gerry.

That was a cool £50,000 each and apparently one of the four was offered £15,000 for his docket the previous day. That is like deciding to swap 50k for 15k but with Rory having a six shot lead there was no way that barter was ever going to happen.

All small change to Rory though. He was lifting the Claret Jug and a cash prize of €1,240,000. Monster money that was hard earned in battling and keeping demons at bay throughout the year and on that particular day.

His third major and the one he craved. The one he mentioned in terms of: 'when I was a kid my putts were to win the Open', when he inadvertently belittled the Ryder Cup. Well now he had realized all those boyhood moments.

What an Open and what a fantastic win for Rory. It was mature and professional. He held a wise Nicklaus and Watson head on his young shoulders. If he keeps doing it that way, he will bottle the ingredients to more success. Spare a thought for two gallants...

Sergio was equally as good from the very start of the tournament to the last. He was determined to get his hands on the jug to make up for the putt that lipped out to Harrington. 'I just lost to the better player, simple as that.' is what he said after.

As for Fowler, not alone is he knocking and banging loudly on all doors; he is maturing like a fine wine. Four rounds sub-60 meant that he became only the third man in history to do that and not win the Open.

Then the celebrations began and Rory was photographed by the world's press all over Hoylake including sitting on the edge of a giant bunker. The selfies began with friends and it was a long day's journey into Liverpool night life. Before he left Hoylake he said:

I'm happy I gave myself a cushion because there were a lot of guys coming at me – especially Sergio and Rickie Fowler. Just to be sitting here and looking at this thing and my name on it is a great feeling. It hasn't sunk in yet and I'm going to enjoy it and let it sink in tonight in the company of my family and friends.

Then the records and the comparisons with the legends of the game and the amount of total majors and so many other things were totted up by the statisticians. Of them all, just one matters and it will be eagerly awaited in the coming years.

If Rory McIlroy wins the US Masters at Augusta in April 2015 – or any Masters between now and the day he puts his clubs away – then he will become only the sixth golfer in history to win the Grand

Slam of all four majors.

On his fantastic day, the words of a great golf writer from the past – Bernard Darwin – are very apt. Inducted into the 'World Golf Hall of Fame', he watched the last of his many Opens at that Liverpool course many decades before.

But on a very blustery evening, as Rory did the rounds with trophy in hand, his famous line rang true almost half a century later:

'Hoylake – blown upon by mighty winds, breeder of mighty champions.'

Chapter 14

EXCELLENCE

In light of Rory's British Open win, another huge and highly illustrious achievement looks very much within his grasp. He could be on course to put himself down in Majors immortality as the first golfer ever to break the all-time record low round.

That currently stands at -9 under 63 and is actually held jointly by Rory and 25 other players – eight of them in the British Open. He shot his 63 at St Andrews in 2010 and also shot 64 there at the Dunhill Links in October 2014.

His length off the tee where he can reach the green with a driver and iron is such that it seems only a matter of time before he shoots 62 or lower at one of the four majors. That is not meant to belittle the weight of history.

It is really incredible that in almost 150 years of majors, only a select group of 26 has reached the magical mark of 63 – and no 62! In that list are the likes of Nicklaus, Player, Miller, Norman, Singh, Olazabal, Stricker and Duffner.

Christy O'Connor Junior was one player who proved a 62 can almost certainly be achieved. At Royal St Georges, Sandwich in 1985, the Irishman broke Sir Henry Cotton's 50-year old course record with 64.

Christy's -8 under round stood for 25 years as the lowest 1st round score in a major until Rory went and broke that with his 1st round 63 in 2010. But Christy faltered over his final few holes at the Kent course. At one stage he was in line for 61 or 62!'

There was to be no hanging about for Rory; no honeymoon period or week away in 'Shangri-La'. Less than two weeks after winning the Open, Rory was back in the US for the Bridgestone Invitational at Akron, Ohio.

On the par-70 Firestone Country Club course, Rory opened with a tame 69 but next day he produced the magic with a -6, 64. Even though he produced another nice sub 70 round with a 66 on Saturday, he trailed Sergio Garcia by two shots with one round remaining.

He was four strokes behind the Spaniard until he birdied the 17th and 18th which was a lovely way for him to end as, from seemingly nowhere, it now put him in with a great chance of victory.

It was a repetition of the Open with the top two fighting it out again in the final group. But not before a 76 minute rain delay on the Sunday which also contributed to a very funny incident.

Russell Henley had lost his playing partner Graham DeLaet, of Canada, who cried off with flu. On the fourth hole Bubba Watson, who was playing with Tiger Woods, spotted Henley on his own and shouted over at him, "Have you no friends?"

Then on the ninth hole, Woods pulled out with back spasms prompting Bubba to say after: 'It was weird – so I'm like, 'I've no friends either' and so I paired up with Russell on the 10th."

McIlroy began the last round in scintillating form. After he birdied five holes in a row from the start, he had cut Sergio's lead of two shots behind to go three shots in front. It was a lead he kept all the way to the chequered flag.

Coincidentally, he eventually ran out a two shot winner on -17 under with Sergio runner-up on -15. It was the exact same score and margin and opponent as Hoylake a fortnight before.

Rory had just won his first ever WGC event. It brought to mind the saying that 'you wait all day for a bus and then two arrive at once'. Two big titles in a row for him, and he also leapt over Adam Scott to regain world number one. Understandably cock-a-hoop he said:

I put some pressure on Sergio early and I rode my luck a little bit on the back nine. Sergio had some putts to get close to me. I had a couple tree limbs that went my way. But I played another really solid round of golf.

He was riding the crest of a wave and before it levelled out to reach the beach sands one big surf remained. It was the last major and one of his favourites, the USPGA. Two days before it began, he was asked to compare his present form with his 2012 USPGA win:

This is better. I'm more in control of my ball, and my ball flight, and mentally I'm really sharp. It's the most comfortable I've ever felt trying to close out a golf tournament there on Sunday. The most pleasing thing was not dwelling on Hoylake but to just keep moving forward. I feel like the way I'm playing that there's a few left in me this year.

In a season blighted by weather delays on the US Tour, the USPGA at Valhalla in Kentucky was not spared. In fact it was to suffer more than most; the damp and dreary conditions, with gloomy overcast skies, seemed to go hand in hand with his start.

Playing with Bubba Watson and Martin Kaymer, he was noticeably struggling. He could not find a spark to ignite anything in his round. Playing the early holes of the back nine, he was still level par for the day.

Then came a flash of lightning and a clatter of thunder, and all hell broke loose. A burst of birdies from the magic wands of McIlroy soon catapulted him into orbit and up on the leaderboard. He struck no less than five birdies in his last seven holes.

The mark of genius, as one moment he was ordinary and in a flash he was sheer class.

A first round 66 was just the start he required and it was almost the best. He lay just a shot behind first round co-leaders Lee Westwood, Kevin Chappell and Ryan Palmer.

Talking to the media afterwards he had this to say about the remarkable turnaround:

I think you have to take whatever you feel inside and turn it into a positive. I was angry and I tried to use that anger as a fuel to propel myself forward. It was great. I think it just shows where my game is mentally right now that I was able to do that.

In the second round the boot was on the other foot as not only did he have to contend with more weather delays, he had to put up with Bubba Watson using foul language throughout the round.

When play began, the golfers were hauled off the course after only around 20 minutes because of torrential downpours. There followed a delay just short of an hour and McIlroy then teed off on the 10th.

After finding a greenside bunker on the par-three 12th, he bogeyed, and he was also struggling with his driving. But birdies followed at 13 and 15 before his round really took off with a brilliant 30ft eagle on the par-five 18th.

This massive bonus meant he had moved to eight under and he now led the USPGA for the first time. Beside him, US Masters champion Bubba was losing his temper and could not hide his feelings or his swearing.

After swinging his tee shot into water, he bellowed out, 'It's fucking bullshit!' before moaning to his caddy about dirt or water on the club face that presumably the caddy should have cleaned off.

Earlier he turned to his trusted lieutenant exclaiming, 'I can't play golf man, I got nothing'. One wonders what Kaymer and McIlroy made of it. Perhaps they wished the Ryder Cup, over a month away, could be held there and then!

Whether it is in amateur or professional sport, you should never let your feelings out. Things like that always inspire the opponent and such was the case with Rory.

An hour later on the par-five, 600-yard seventh hole, his three wood came to rest 10 feet from the pin.

He missed the eagle but having dropped a shot at the second, he got it back there and earned interest on his efforts with another birdie at the ninth, his final hole. At the halfway stage, McIlroy led the USPGA by a single shot from Jim Furyk and Jason Day.

His reaction to leading the USPGA was:

The course was pretty wet so the ball was not rolling anywhere.

When it is not raining it is very playable and you can make scores. I didn't get off to the best of starts but I righted the ship and caught fire around the turn. I am happy with 67. I am feeling good about my game and feeling confident. I am hitting the ball well but not as well as yesterday. I was still in really good control of my game and my emotions and I need to do that over the weekend as well.

Conditions were so bad that Shane Lowry, who made the cut at even par, made a complaint to referee John Paramor. There was mist everywhere with water on greens and fairways. He in turn radioed the top brass but the order barked back was 'proceed'.

On moving day, Rory moved to -13 after another 67. He had maintained his lead and his brilliant form. It was his third successive sub-60 round and since his missed cut at the Irish Open, it was his 13th in his last 15 rounds played which was just an incredible streak.

Going into that final round he held a slim shot lead from little-known Austrian surprise package Bernd Weisberger, who in turn was a shot in front of Rickie Fowler. A further shot back on -10 was Mickelson and Day, with Stenson and Oosthuizen on nine under.

So he was still in front but only just. As he looked in his rear view mirror, he saw a host of the world's greatest golfers trying to overtake him. Pass him they would – and not just one.

****

Yet again, and before play even started in the final round of the 65th USPGA, the siren echoed all round Valhalla to signal another weather delay. A monsoon dumped just over an inch of rain within minutes and it resulted in a suspension of almost two hours.

All the waiting around in the dampness did not do Rory any good. Once again, and just like on the first tee at Hoylake, he looked nervous as well. You would have thought pars at the first two holes would have been just the tonic to settle him but then panic set in.

When he bogeyed the third hole after three-putting, he was joined at the top by no less than four other golfers on -12. He then bogeyed the sixth after finding the greenside bunker and although he got that shot back at the par-five seventh, he was overtaken at the top.

Henrik Stenson was in electrifying form and he was later joined by Ricky Fowler and Phil Mickcslon. In fact, Stenson's putter would fire him to -15 and a whopping three shots ahead of Rory.

McIlroy had to stop the rot. He needed something to happen but more importantly, he needed to make something happen. With nothing to lose he had to push the boat out. The holes were running out as he hit the back nine.

Shaking himself together and with pure determination he created absolute magic on the 10th hole. It will long live in the memory. A perfect drive of over 300 yards left him with just over 280 to the pin.

If you did not see his shot at the time, then get out your PC and google the words 'Rory's shot to the 10th hole in USPGA'. You will see one of the finest fairway woods ever recorded in the history of the game.

Standing in the middle of the course, with knees slightly bent and eyes firmly focussed on the ball, Rory takes a full swing and sends the ball out left. It is a dangerous ploy. You have to have practised this shot thousands of times to get it right, and so there is no fluke.

He also hits it left as the pin on the green is tucked away in the back left. If he goes straight or right, not only does he gamble with troublesome bunkers but he knows he will leave his ball too far from the pin if it makes the green. He must go for it – and go left.

The ball rockets from his feet like a surface to air missile and it tears along the left side of the rough like a city bus travelling briskly along a bus lane. It comes into land and hits the fairway only narrowly avoiding the rough.

It skirts along the edge of the fairway and then you can hear a roar go up from the galleries up ahead. They see that it has not only approached the front of the green but it is still travelling fast.

Like a laser-guided missile homing in on the target, all of a sudden you can see the ball nearing the pin. The roar reaches an almighty crescendo. The ball comes to a stop no more than eight feet from the flag. He duly sank the eagle putt to get to -14, a shot behind.

At the 11th he had a good chance for birdie to draw level with the leaders but had to settle for par three. Then at the par-four 13th, he birdied and incredibly he was back as joint leader with Phil Mickelson at -15 under as Stenson dropped away.

The turning point came at the 16th and it did not actually involve Rory. Mickelson got into trouble off the tee and although he tried gallantly to salvage the situation with a 10-foot putt for par, he missed to drop back to -14.

Still there was more drama to be played out. Seeing and hearing of Phil's mistake, Rory could have played the percentages like he did so admirably in the Open. But with two holes left there was a huge reason why he did not.

Rory knew there was a good chance that because of that error, Phil would birdie the par-five 18th to finish his tournament on -15. However, there was no guarantee that Rory would birdie it meaning then that there would be a playoff between him and Lefty.

The thing about a very reachable par five is that on average it is 50/50 you will birdie, and at best 60/40. So there is never any guarantee as most golfers have to put extra effort into the drive, which can often go awry.

With that very much to the forefront of his mind, Rory pushed the boat out on the 17th. He hit a magnificent shot over 300 yards – but it found a bunker! As that was happening, Phil did indeed birdie the final hole to finish as the leader in the clubhouse at -15 under.

But Rory hit such a long drive that all he was hoping for as he walked down the fairway was to see his ball in a good lie in the sand. He was in luck. With just 150 yards to the green, he hit his second shot to 11 feet for a birdie chance.

He rammed it home and now at -16, all he had to do was precisely the same as in Liverpool. Take a stroll in the park up the 18th and acknowledge the applause from the crowds as the 2014 USPGA winner. It was that easy and that's precisely what happened.

A routine par five with no histrionics won Rory his second major and third title in a month. It was also his fourth major in all by the age of 25. In near darkness, everything was hurried in regard to the presentation ceremonies and that took a little gloss off his great win.

When he sank the winning putt, he turned and punched the air in an action that looked like he was throwing a javelin at a major athletics meet. Thrilled and beaming with a smile that never left his face, it was his happiest moment in golf as he revealed:

I really gutted it out today. The other three [major wins] were quite comfortable but I really had to dig deep today. It's been just incredible. I didn't think in my wildest dreams I'd have a summer like this. I've played the best golf of my life.

He did, and he played the greatest shot of his life which by a long way eclipsed his 'stone dead' pitch to the par three in his first major win at Congressional. The fairway wood for eagle at the 10th is also right up there with the greatest shots ever witnessed.

Although unquestionably it won him that fourth major, and so it will always be, to this point, his greatest shot, he still had work to do to win. So it was not a crowning glory 18th hole shot to rival Christy O'Connor Junior or Padraig Harrington's spectaculars.

But it is unquestionably right there in the middle of the top 10 shots of all time behind those just mentioned (with Christy number one) and a few of Mickelson's. Get the clip out again Rory: just like Christy and Padraig's, one never tires of such shots – strokes of genius.

One sublime moment on the 10th changed everything and in the immortal words of the American commentator as the last putt dropped, 'IT'S GLORY FOR RORY IN KENTUCKY'.

Chapter 15

FROM EAGLES TO GLENEAGLES

Just because the last major of the 2014 season was done, dusted and put away in Rory's cupboard, it did not mean that his season was over. Far from it – he had two huge prizes still to play for.

First up was the series of Fedex Cup events, with each of the four tournaments carrying a first prize the equal of any of the four majors – over $1.4 million leading to a possible $10 million bonus to the overall winner.

Rory was gutted to lose out on winning it in 2012 having been runner-up to Brandt Snedeker, and he will desperately want to have this title on his resume in the coming years. He also knows that a certain Tiger Woods holds two Fedex titles.

Then at the end of September Rory would jet to Scotland to team up with his European colleagues for the Ryder Cup. Rory has two from two Ryder Cups in his bag while also having a good personal record in the event. Lee Westwood's career points will be his target.

On the 21 August, he teed off in round one of the Fedex Cup at The Barclays held in New Jersey's Ridgewood Country Club. There is quite a large Irish-American population in these parts so he was not lacking in support.

But he got off to a very poor start shooting a +3, 74 and although he improved next day with a -6, 65 the damage had been done. That score only really got him back into it and two further rounds of 70 was nowhere near good enough to trouble Hunter Mahan.

The American, who had famously beaten Rory in the final of the World Matchplay, opened with 66 and rounded off his week with 65 to win on 14 under. Rory finished tied 22nd on five under and at least he could try to improve on this in the overall Fedex competition.

This he most certainly did at the Tournament Players Club (TPC) in Boston the following week. Roared by another hugely partisan 'Irish' crowd, once again he did not get off to a great start after posting a -1, 70.

He steadily improved with a 69 in the second round and after dazzling the crowds with a fantastic 64 in the penultimate round, he had put himself right back into the mix with a chance of winning his third US Tour title in little over a month.

Another 70 was a huge disappointment as Chris Kirk went on to win by two shots. Rory came in fifth and despite lamenting the lackluster final round display he was now a leading contender for the Fedex jackpot. All he required from two remaining events was a win.

The show traveled on to Colorado a week later for the BMW Championship at Cherry Hills Country club. Three great rounds were ruined by another gut wrenching round which cost him a shot at winning.

After recording a pair of 67s, he was stopped in his tracks in the third round with a 72. Rory will wince at what befell him during that event. His saga at the par-three 12th hole will be recorded forever as one of his most infamous moments on a golf course.

To gauge what happened and how embarrassing it was, measure out a distance of four feet five inches on your floor. That is how far Rory left his ball from the pin after a stunning shot left him with an easy birdie opportunity.

Well it looked easy, but in sport we all know nothing is certain. Approaching his ball Rory must have felt he was going to get a shot back on his scorecard. He had bogeyed three holes and birdied two and was one over for his round. This would get him back to six under.

He missed and he missed again....and again and finally he put the ball in the hole with his fourth putt! It was excruciating agony. Coming into the 12th on five under, he left it falling back to three under.

The 200-yard hole can be treacherous if the pin is placed at the back of the green where it is situated on an undulating sloping surface. But there were no excuses for taking four putts and so it was totally unforgivable when he did almost exactly the same thing next day!

Leaving his ball just over 20 feet for birdie, he again took four putts and dropped two shots. Although he got them back and retrieved his round with a 66 to tie eighth, it was too little, too late. Billy Horschel won by two shots and was one of only five men in line for Fedex glory.

With just the Tour Championship in the deep south of Atlanta, Georgia, remaining, Horschel, Rory, Hunter Mahan, Chris Kirk and Jim Furyk had been the most consistent performers. Whoever triumphed in the final event would be richly rewarded.

Going into the climactic week of the series, for which 130 golfers started and it was now whittled down to a final 30, Rory caused another ripple of laughter and put a few smiles on faces when he again referred to his darting home for a day or two. He explained:

It's amazing what a night in your own bed can do. I was standing in the shower in Denver [BMW in Colorado] on Monday and I just thought to myself 'why am I traveling to Atlanta today'. So I didn't and I went home to Florida for a day and a half!

He had plenty more to say at the obligatory eve of tournament press conference and with regard to possibly winning the Fedex Cup for the first time. He said:

Of course $10 million is a lot of money to anyone and I'm not saying I'm not motivated by money in any way. But winning the FedEx Cup is one of the things I haven't achieved in the game of golf. And that's the real reason I want to win this week. The title would mean more to me.

Elaborating on this he added:

Anything other than a win would be a disappointment. Although if I came second or third and still ended up winning, that would be cool as well. But I want to win as I only have to beat 28 other guys [one withdrew through injury] rather than a regular field of 155.

It was also the first time for 22 years that the final event did not contain either Tiger or Phil Mickelson. With regard to that, Rory then made one of his most controversial remarks in quite some time when stating:

Phil is 44 and Tiger nearly 40 so they're obviously getting into the last few holes of their careers. That's what happens. It obviously gets harder as you get older. I'll be able to tell you in 20 years how it feels.

When the comments flew around the world in a matter of minutes, Rory later back-tracked and explained that he meant Tiger was plagued with injuries and Phil was in a bad patch of form.

He also said that he would say this to them regularly in the locker room and that he was only stating facts. But these sort of needless remarks, as mentioned in the first book, have a nasty habit of coming back to bite hard in future.

At East Lake Golf Club on 11th September, Rory frustratingly began with another poor first round when signing for a -1, 69. At least the old freaky Friday syndrome had been firmly banished when he improved greatly next day with a 65.

That put him right up there in contention but at the halfway stage one of the five was effectively out of it. Hunter Mahan was all over the place on the golf course and was enduring a nightmare. His chances faded fast.

McIlroy could see Las Vegas-like casino lights flashing *'Jackpot $11 million dollars'* as he hit the front in the third round, courtesy of a 67 which put him at the top on nine under, but it was a case of the cream rising.

Joining him on nine under under was Billy Horschel and just behind in the top half dozen was Chris Kirk and Jim Furyk. All were hungry hombres looking to swell their already bulging bank balances. It all promised to be a fascinating and intriguing last day shootout.

Horschel and McIlroy paired together in the final group of the final round of the final Fedex event. There seemed on paper to be only one winner. But it turned out very different to how almost everybody envisaged beforehand.

The gritty American actually seemed more relaxed and his early birdies seemed to unsettle Rory. It went from bad to worse for him when he racked up a horror double bogey on the fifth.

Needing to make something happen quickly, he tried to put more length into his drive on the ninth and it ended up almost out of bounds beside a fence. A microphone picked up the discussion between him and his caddy J P Fitzgerald:

JP: *'Just hit it over the bushes….chip it back on the fairway for your third.'*

Rory: *'Nah, I'm just going to have a go and see where it ends up.'*

It was the wrong choice but he did well to come out of it with just a bogey.

Then at the very next hole, the putting fiasco came back to haunt him again. His second shot drew applause for finishing inside 20 feet from the pin and a possible birdie. But he took three putts to get down for yet another bogey.

On the 11th he racked up his third bogey in a row and by this stage the wheels had come off. Down to four under, he was well behind the leaders and it was a case of trying to rescue some pride.

To his credit he finished with three birdies in a row on 15, 16 and 17 to finish with a +1, 71. He climbed back up to join Jim Furyk in a tie for second on eight under, which was three shots behind the winner and new Fedex Cup champion, Billy Horschel. The final Fedex standings were:

1.	Billy Horschel	4750 points	$10,000,000
2.	Chris Kirk	3100 points	$3,000,000
3.	Rory McIlroy	3050 points	$2,000,000

The Irish Times golf correspondent Philip Reid put it very well in his report next day. His opening paragraph read:

Rory McIlroy punched the wrong numbers into the ATM in the final round of the Tour Championship as he failed to cash in on the FedEx Cup's $10 million bonus payout.

As for Rory it seemed that his brilliant season ended in a sort of payback time and he also hinted at exhaustion when saying:

I'm disappointed. I made too many bogeys early on and I just didn't have the energy to get myself back up after that. When I did try, my putter let me down. So it was disappointing but I'm glad I finished well and made those birdies to get myself back up to a fairly respectable finish. So yeah, a little disappointing but overall I've had a great season.

Europe's Ryder Cup Captain Paul McGinley on hearing of Rory's words probably wanted him to get home to his Florida bed as soon as possible. He wanted a fighting-fit, fresh and raring-to-go Rory for the Ryder Cup a few weeks later.

****

As far back as 2004, and before Paul McGinley ever registered on most people's radars to become a future Ryder Cup Captain, I knew that one day he was going to be appointed to that role. It was all thanks to some insider information from Christy O'Connor Junior.

When I met with Christy in his former apartment at City West Golf Club back then, he expressed his disgust that in the entire history of the Ryder Cup, there had never been an Irish captain.

Being a freelance journalist, I wanted to go to the press with this information and a story to the effect *'Christy Junior Appeals for McGinley Captaincy'* but Christy swore me to secrecy and asked that I leave it for him to reveal in his future autobiography. I agreed.

For one reason and another, it took the pair of us eight years to get his book out and without going into his several pages of disgust on that 'anti-Irish' subject this is a flavor of what he wrote in July 2012. In the chapter entitled 'An Irish Jersey' he stated:

Why have all the various Ryder Cup Committees down through the years not made some of these great Irishmen a Ryder Cup Captain? That is a very serious question that needs to be asked.

It is high time we ask it and get answers because it cannot go on like that. The 2006 event in Ireland was the perfect opportunity to appoint an Irish Captain. It would have been almost like a 13th man on the team. That was an opportunity shamefully missed.

Many years ago there was another Irish venue short-listed for the hosting of a Ryder Cup. The final decision came down to Lord Derby who had the casting vote. It was no surprise that Ireland lost it.

A long line of disgraceful wrongs can now be finally put right. I am sure that I am not alone in asking and appealing to the current Ryder Cup Committee to select Paul McGinley as the next Ryder Cup Captain for 2014.

Everyone saw how hugely popular Paul was when his team-mates flung him into the lake complete with tricolour after he holed the winning putt at the K Club. He was overlooked for the Captaincy before when he was made 2010 Vice Captain instead.

After he assists Ollie again in 2012, if Paul is not made Captain and this injustice continues then we know without any shadow of doubt that the selection committee are anti-Irish. Some of their reasoning just does not make sense either.

When I was bidding for it in 2004 - and I campaigned very hard with Sean Quinn - they turned me down on the grounds that a major winner should Captain the side. I have never heard such rubbish.

Sam Torrance never won a major and Mark James made one of the biggest balls-ups when he lost a huge lead to the Americans. I am absolutely disgusted with the attitudes and I have continually watched this go on since my uncle (Christy O'Connor Senior) was snubbed. He was never once asked to be Captain.

This was despite the fact that both Dai Rees and Bernard Hunt went on to lead the side on several occasions. With respect to those two great players they were nowhere near the level of my uncle.

The last word on the subject must concern the huge bands of loyal Irish golf followers. It is a huge miscarriage of justice on them. They have supported the Ryder Cup in every corner of the globe with the tricolour everywhere to be seen. It's a disgrace.

Paul McGinley was officially ratified as European Ryder Cup Captain on Tuesday, January 15th, 2013. His appointment was met with delight by players and fans alike as he was as popular as Ollie.

2010 Captain Colin Montgomerie who put in a late bid said 'we'll all get behind Paul now and we wish him well' while Graeme McDowell summed up the feelings of most everybody saying "thoughtful, articulate, prepared, motivated, fair and respected."

Rory immediately sent out his own personal message of congratulations but also with a side swipe at those who dared to think of appointing Montgomerie at the 11th hour. His tweet read:

Common sense prevailed in the end...Paul McGinley Ryder Cup Captain!!! I couldn't be happier for him. Roll on Gleneagles.

McGinley had finally become the first (and long overdue) Irish Ryder Cup Captain in the long history of the event. He sank the winning putt at The Belfry in 2002 and had never lost as a player, Captain or Vice-Captain in nine previous Ryder Cup or Seve Trophy matches.

With 'Monty' in the melting pot, McGinley was relieved and ecstatic to get the job. It certainly helped that he had the unanimous support of the players. On his appointment he was so dignified in revealing what he would have said had he not been made Captain:

I had notes in my pocket about how I was going to project myself and what I was going to do. I assured George O'Grady and Richard Hills that I would act with integrity expected by the Tour. So if it wasn't going to be me, I would wish the winner the best of luck and leave it at that knowing that it was probably my last opportunity.

On Tuesday 2 September 2014 after the final 'counting' event at the Italian Open, he announced his team to face the Americans at Gleneagles on 26th September. He dropped Luke Donald and brought in Scotland's Stephen Gallacher as one of his three wildcards.

His team was: Rory McIlroy, Henrik Stenson, Victor Dubuisson, Jamie Donaldson, Sergio Garcia, Thomas Bjorn, Justin Rose, Martin Kaymer and Graeme McDowell, and his three wildcards (the old system was two) were Ian Poulter, Stephen Gallacher and Lee Westwood.

Forty-seven year old McGinley began the 40th Ryder Cup by putting out Rory and Sergio Garcia in the very first match of the

'Morning Fourballs' at 7.30 am. They faced Phil Mickelson and Keegan Bradley who had a fine and unbeatable record from Medinah.

The media actually tried to stir things up by using Mickelson's tongue-in-cheek remarks which insinuated that Europe, McIlroy and McDowell could be affected by the apparent disharmony between Rory and Graeme over various issues. McDowell had stated:

Everyone knows that there are well documented personal issues between myself and Rory over the past couple of years and now that he is world number one and the big star, the dynamic between myself and Rory has changed for ever.

At Medinah a couple of years ago – and Rory and I spoke about this – I found the better ball format very difficult with him because he likes to go first, I let him at it, and I kind of come second.

You know, he's standing there beating it 350 down the middle, and I put my tee in the ground thinking there's not really a lot of point in me hitting this tee shot and find myself throwing myself at it, and literally it kind of didn't help my game much at Medinah playing better-ball with him.

Foursomes I think is different. I think we could still play foursomes really well together.

Rory actually responded to this by saying that at the pre-Ryder Cup dinner, he and G-Mac had a go at Mickelson in jest saying 'we're going to call in the FBI!' This referred to part of Phil Mickelson's financial affairs which are currently being investigated by the FBI.

It all made for an intriguing match where Mickelson and Bradley had the last laugh. They won on the very last hole after an inspired display from Bradley. He took the match by the scruff of the neck with brilliant winning approaches on 17 and 18.

McIlroy was visibly disconsolate as he took off his cap afterwards and on the way off the green he had his head down. The Americans went on from this and by the end of the morning, they held a 2 ½ - 1 ½ point lead.

The Captain sent Rory out with Sergio again for the 'Afternoon Foursomes' but this time in the last match against Ricky Fowler and Jimmy Walker. Things went from bad to worse for Europe and for

Rory as the American pairing were giving them a real lesson.

Although America's lead had been turned upside down and into a 4 ½ - 2 ½ deficit, Fowler and Walker were playing well and as the last match out on the course, they were 2-up with just 17 and 18 to play.

It looked like they would cut the gap to just a point overnight but then came some Rory magic when it was needed most. Garcia left his ball 34 feet from the pin for birdie on 17 and Rory calmly sank the monster putt. They were one down with just the last to play.

With their dander up, Rory teed up his ball and you could see from his stance that he was priming himself for one of his boomers. He let loose but then winced as he saw his ball shoot out to the right towards a forest.

He got lucky. His ball hit a pine tree and at just short of 300 yards, it plumped down in the light rough and was sitting up nicely. Garcia then took out a five wood and knocked the ball to within 15 feet of the flag.

The roars bellowed out as Rory and Sergio pumped their fists together and a few minutes later all hell broke loose as Europe won the hole. They secured a precious half point to win the afternoon games by a whopping three points to a half point. Rory was very relieved:

I'm really happy. Sergio's shot was fantastic and you know, if we'd lost both matches today I don't know how I'd have felt. It would have been very hard to take especially after all the work put in and then to get nothing out of it. But to get a half point feels as good as a win and that's fantastic for the team. I'm happy.

On Saturday morning Rory was out again but this time with another change of partner. As had been expected in the days before the Cup there would be no Graeme McDowell, as Rory was paired with 'Mr Ryder Cup' Ian Poulter versus Rickie Fowler & Jimmy Walker.

However the pair could not find a spark to ignite a win and in the end they looked on anxiously as it all came down to Ricky Fowler on the last hole. He had an eagle putt from 12 feet to win the match but it slid by. Rory was again relieved to 'win' a half point.

There were three big talking points from that Saturday. The score had been a carbon copy of the previous day. America won the morning session each day by 2 ½ - 1 ½ and Europe were revitalized in the afternoon to win 3 ½ - ½ meaning they held a 10-6 overnight lead.

Rory and Sergio were reunited that afternoon and they finally recorded a sweet victory as they enjoyed a relatively easy 3 and 2 win against Hunter Mahan and Jim Furyk. Rory having started out a little rusty on Friday morning was visibly getting better and better.

So too were his team, but the major story from that day concerned Justin Rose who was involved in one of the greatest games ever seen in the history of golf, never mind the Ryder Cup.

Rose and Stenson came back from an early deficit to absolutely blitz their American opponents Bubba Watson and Matt Kuchar. They struck no less than 10 birdies in a row – with Rose recording seven of them - from the seventh hole to the 16th. It broke all Cup records.

Two-down through six holes, Henrik Stenson birdied the seventh and when Justin Rose followed with birdie on eight, the match was all square. Rose then birdied nine, 10 and 11; Stenson birdied 12; Rose the 13th; Stenson the 14th and Rose the next two to win on the 16th 3 and 2.

Meanwhile there was bad blood developing in Camp America as Mickelson and Bradley were dropped. In the case of Mickelson, it did seem very harsh as he has a history of righting wrongs from a previous day. It was also his first full sit out in his 20 year career.

So to the final day, and although there were reminders and warnings about Medinah and Brookline where 10-6 deficits had been overturned before, Europe were the overwhelming favourites.

Eyebrows were raised with veteran Captain Tom Watson's formation. To see rookies Jordan Spieth and Patrick Reed lead out America ahead of more all round form and experienced players was baffling.

Surely Tom knew that the two young lads were bound to face the might of a Rose, Poulter, McDowell or McIlroy. Personally speaking, the night before I tried to pit my wits with his selection and I wrote down Mahan and Walker first and second – both won points.

The tone was set early on when Rory McIlroy won Europe's first point as he battered poor Ricky Folwer into submission with a stunning birdie barrage. When top man Jordan Spieth, 3-up, was pegged back by McDowell and lost 2 and 1, it was curtains.

Winning 13 ½ - 9 ½ it all came down to Wales Jamie Donaldson who was 4-up on Keegan Bradley. He spurned one opportunity to win the Ryder Cup when missing a 12-foot putt but then won it with a stunning approach that sat two feet from the pin.

At that moment, the Cup was won. McGinley rushed out on the course and almost hit Tom Watson! He then walked alongside Tom and as they made their way to the green with the European contingent in tow, the Captain and Bradley conceded the win.

A little while later, Rory grabbed Donaldson with both of his hands behind his head and shaking him wildly screamed into his eyes in sheer delight: 'What an iron! You boyo-oooooooo.'

If Medinah was the making of Ian Poulter then unbeaten Justin Rose, who was also an unsung hero there, was the golfer of the tournament at Gleneagles. His ball striking, blitzing of pins and sinking of putts was one of the finest Ryder Cup performances.

From an American point of view, Hunter Mahan is quality. He was 4-up on Justin Rose and but for an uncharacteristic error on the 18th, would have burst Justin's bubble rather than shake hands on a half. His first major is nigh.

Despite the fallout and bickering – and we can only hope Tom Watson will be afforded the respect he deserves – America and Tom had a huge part to play. That was also reflected upon at every opportunity by a class human being in Paul McGinley.

Several times McGinley said 'Let's not forget America' and when he was asked for his highlight of the whole event, a measure of his stature was in his reply: 'Walking down the 18th and sharing experiences with Tom Watson – as well as Europe winning.'

Rory referred to McGinley afterwards in terms of being 'thoughtful' in almost every facet of Ryder Cup details – from statistics to organization to the discussions and jottings in the team room – as his huge strengths.

Rory also said that McGinley had put everything into his two years. Going a step further, I'd venture to say he was the greatest Captain in Ryder Cup history – not because of this attention to detail – but due to his 'thoughtfulness'.

He gave every single person his time before, during and after the event. Newspaper interviews, broadcast interviews, private functions, chat shows, public appearances – he wore it all with a beaming smile full of verve. A beautiful man who deserved to win.

Rory, who was seen spraying large bottles of bubbly 'Grand Prix-style' over his teammates, now held a 100% record of three wins from his first three Cup appearances and more personal points accumulated. Looking back on the week he reflected:

He [McGinley] has just been the most wonderful Captain and I cannot speak highly enough of him. From the first day we got here the speeches he gave, the videos he showed, the people he got to talk to us and the imagery in the team room – it all tied in together.

When he said after his fourth major win, 'This is the greatest summer of my life', he was not to know then that Ryder Cup success was just around the corner. It was a fitting end and glorious top up to his summer of '14 – and in that top up he revealed something else:

I couldn't have asked for the summer to end any better. I didn't know that it had not been done since 1977 but, you know, if it's not me in a couple years time again, then I hope it's one of these guys [his team-mates] that gets two Majors and gets a Ryder Cup.

****

It is now a race to be 'Sixth Man Slam' – will it be Rory, who requires the Masters, or Lefty, who needs the US open, who will follow the greats into immortality by winning the Grand Slam?

And for Rory, after the BBC Sports Personality of The Year award, there will be many more years of chasing Majors and competing in Ryder Cups.

An entire sporting world awaits the ultimate glory for Rory. It could be a short road, or it may be a long road, but we his passengers will venture along for that thrilling ride.